Sincerest greetings
& good wishes to one
who loves the little white
schoolhouse from the
writer.

E. F. Hartford

10-21-77

The Little White Schoolhouse

ELLIS FORD HARTFORD

THE UNIVERSITY PRESS OF KENTUCKY

Research for The Kentucky Bicentennial Bookshelf
is assisted by a grant from the
National Endowment for the Humanities.
Views expressed in the Bookshelf do not
necessarily represent those of the Endowment.

ISBN: 0-8131-0231-6

Library of Congress Catalog Card Number: 76-46028

A statewide cooperative scholarly publishing agency
serving Berea College, Centre College of Kentucky,
Eastern Kentucky University, The Filson Club,
Georgetown College, Kentucky Historical Society,
Kentucky State University, Morehead State University,
Murray State University, Northern Kentucky University,
Transylvania University, University of Kentucky,
University of Louisville, and Western Kentucky University.

Editorial and Sales Offices: Lexington, Kentucky 40506

To all Kentuckians who
lived and learned and loafed and loved
in the little white schoolhouse

Contents

Preface

FEW INSTITUTIONS have been held in such fond regard and recalled in such nostalgic terms as the little red schoolhouse. It ranks with the old oaken bucket, the little brown church in the vale, and the pictures of the old home place that millions of people have carried in that "inward eye" mentioned by Wordsworth on that long-past spring day. But the Kentucky common schoolhouses were not painted red as were those of New England; they were mostly white, if not of unpainted log construction. And it was not the simple little boxlike schoolhouse itself that earned all that fond affection. What happened on the way to and from school, on the playground, and within the school walls are all treasured in the memory banks of former pupils in much the same manner as families recall their happy evenings around the fireside or those trips to grandmother's house for Thanksgiving.

But the little white schoolhouse is gone, along with the simple agrarian way of life that characterized the people of the neighborhood to which it belonged. Thoughtful people realize what has been lost in the passing of this institution and of the values that best characterized its time and place. It may be found that there was far more to the little white schoolhouse and the neighborhood surrounding it than is suggested by mere nostalgic recollections and remembrances of former pupils. Perhaps it is pertinent to suggest that Americans might well seek some of the same strengths and values in their diverse pattern of communities that were enjoyed by our ancestors of the old rural-agrarian way of life. We might also strive to obtain schools that fit and belong to their respective communities as did the little white schoolhouse.

Acknowledgments

SPECIAL THANKS are due my colleagues who provided much assistance in the Margaret I. King Library at the University of Kentucky: Dr. Jacqueline Bull, Miss Kate T. Irvine, and Mrs. Mary A. Sullivan. Also very helpful were the library and archives staffs of the Filson Club, the Kentucky Historical Society, and the state Department of Records and Archives. Typing and xeroxing assistance for early drafts of this book was provided by the Kentucky Research Foundation.

The assistance of a good number of graduate students in history of education classes and seminars at the University of Kentucky who helped interview former pupils of one-room schools is gratefully acknowledged. These classes were held in the 1950s and early 1970s. Consequently if any names have been omitted, this is the result of human frailty and not of intentional discourtesy. Names are listed as recorded in class rolls despite later changes in marital status, acquisition of advanced degrees, and the like: John Atkins, Olive E. Barrett, Gloria Batts, James T. Biliter, Gene Bonny, Anita B. Boyle, Aleene Brown, Norcia T. Brown, Ellen Cameron, Henrietta Jane Castle, Carletta Chaney, Marilyn Clark, Vicki Lynn Collins, Josephine Connell, George A. Cordell, Ralph E. Drake, Evelyn Myers Edwards, Mary Bruce Farley, Jean Ramery Fraley, Thelma B. Garner, Della Mae Goins, Carol Sue Hammons, Shirley Hatfield, Lois Hutchins, Kay L. Isaacs, Brenda Jenkins, David Jenks, Charles E. Jinks, Anita Jones, Eloise Kendrick, Sister Susan Kilb, S.C.N., Juanita Kurtz, Robbie C. Langford, Nellie Lawrence, Florence Martin, Nancy H.

Mason, Doris Mays, Ann Milburn, Sarah W. Miller, Susan Montgomery, Gloria Morris, Mary Lloyd Nichols, Pat Nickell, Herbert B. Popplewell, Sandy Slone Pratt, Virginia Schneider, Alberta Smith, Linda Smith, Don Snyder, William O. Sprinkle, John Gay Stringer, John Dennis Sullivan, Pauline Sweazy, Ann Tandy, William A. Tucker, Julia D. Voelker, Sister Elizabeth Wehri, and William Wireman.

I am also indebted to two teachers of one-room schools still in service in the 1970s: Mrs. Helen Martin of Daniels Creek School in Floyd County and Mr. Fred Boggs of Otter Creek School in Perry County.

Finally I wish to thank the great number of former pupils and teachers of old-time common schools who have shared their experiences with me in both oral and written reminiscences.

1

COMMON SCHOOLS OF COMMON PEOPLE

THE OLD-TIME COMMON SCHOOL was truly the school of the people. For nearly a century the rude log cabins and their successors, the little white schoolhouses, provided the typical school experience for the great majority of Kentuckians. This common school belonged to the people of the neighborhood. Nearly everyone had some connection with it—as taxpayer (without any enthusiasm), as voter in trustee's elections, as visitor or participant in social and public functions held in the schoolhouse, as trustee, as volunteer when repairs or improvements were made, or as patron after having been a pupil in one's early years. People could truly feel and say, "This is our school." They built it or managed to get it constructed; they elected neighbors as trustees, men they knew and trusted, with whom they could communicate and deal; and they felt free to use it for meetings and other purposes of interest to the people of the "deestrict."

The common schools that served the people came about only after lengthy and arduous efforts. Nearly thirty years of statehood passed before there was any success in establishing schools for the children of the common folk.

During that early period, from 1792 to 1821, there had

been one official and various unofficial kinds of effort for schools. In earliest pioneer days, "fort schools" were conducted in some stockades to provide the merest rudiments of learning for children of the settlers. These schools operated only when an adult who could teach was available and when parents were concerned enough to subscribe to the support of such opportunity for their children.

After settlers were able to live out on their newly won lands, schools were established where local leaders believed in formal schooling and took the initiative in getting parents to support subscription schools for their neighborhoods. A good number of schools began to operate in many neighborhoods under various kinds of sponsorship. Some were established by a leading citizen who would enlist other parents in support of a school; others were initiated by town officials, church groups, and by groups of parents banding together to arrange for a teacher to instruct their sons and daughters. These "neighborhood schools" were the expression of the traditional British (and Virginian) view that parents were responsible for the education of their offspring. Only in cases of indigent or orphaned children would provisions be made by the parish authorities. In the daughter Commonwealth—where church and state were clearly separated—this responsibility was exercised by the county courts, which arranged for the necessary care and instruction by means of apprenticeship to responsible adults for both practical experience in a trade and tuition in the "three Rs."

But during the first twenty-nine years of statehood the only legal provision for public education was that of land-grants for county academies or seminaries which would afford instruction in the higher branches to those scholars who were in a position to take advantage of this opportunity. Sponsors of the county academies expected that there would be enough graduates to provide qualified teachers for the various neighborhood schools. Most of the county academies soon used up their resources and faded away, however, and the need for schools open to all became increasingly evident to many leaders at both state and local levels.

In 1821 the legislature enacted the Literary Fund Act, which authorized funds for schools in districts to be established by the several county courts, but later legislatures reneged on the arrangement. The next step (in 1825) was legislation to encourage the establishment of private schools by groups of five or more persons who could obtain charters and operate schools. This was followed by "permissive" school legislation (1830) that authorized citizens of districts to vote taxes upon themselves for local schools. These ineffective acts and numerous other efforts for legislation for schools occupied most of the 1820s and 1830s. It was clear that the legislature sought a system that would cost as little as possible; it was equally clear that almost any plan for financing the needed schools other than by taxes levied directly by the legislature would be acceptable.

In 1838, after the United States Congress placed surplus treasury funds on deposit in the several states to be used for education and internal improvements, backers of public schools were able to get the Common Schools Act through the General Assembly. Then followed a dozen years of dedicated effort by state and local leaders to get schools actually established. This period of the 1840s was also marked by bitter struggles to save the School Fund so newly gained and to protect the common school system by provisions in the new constitution of 1850.

The 1850s were a decade of growth and progress, but the 1860s brought the Civil War and near-disaster for the common schools. After the war there came some twenty-five years of rebuilding—to get schools open again with added public support, and to establish schools for children of the freedmen.

In 1893 the fourth (and present) constitution placed

3

responsibility for "an efficient system of schools" upon the legislature. The comprehensive Common School Act of the same year provided the basis for operation of common schools during the period that might be considered their heyday. In the next fifteen years to 1908 the number of "deestrict" schools reached a total of some 8,500 —7,400 and 1,100 in white and colored districts respectively. Some 25,000 trustees were responsible for the operation of the schools for the vast majority of pupils of school age.

During this period the school law required trustees to visit all parents during the fortnight prior to opening of school to urge upon them the necessity of having their children of school age attend regularly. Those trustees who took this duty seriously knew in advance what kinds of people they would visit—farm families for the most part.

The Commonwealth entered the twentieth century substantially the rural, agrarian state it had been throughout most of its history. An overwhelming majority of over two million Kentuckians resided in rural homes, worked a quarter-million farms, held to agrarian values. Most lived on their own land, but approximately one-third were tenants or renters. Farmers of affluence had tenant families on their farms and possibly one or more hired hands.

Even in most towns and villages, agriculture was a major factor in the life and prosperity of most inhabitants. Pupils from the homes of the blacksmith, the gristmiller, and the crossroads grocer knew the same attitudes, language patterns, and skills as those from the farms. So did many from the homes that depended upon the coal-mining and logging enterprises of Eastern and Western Kentucky, for most miners and loggers of that time came from rural backgrounds. And a great many of the business and professional men of the cities had grown up on farms.

The life-style of most families that patronized the

4

common school was generally rural, agrarian, conservative, individualistic, and based on the puritan ethic. In the characteristic modest frame houses of the state lived families with several children, whose food and other necessities came largely from their own fields, forests, and livestock, and whose ideas and values were much the same as those handed on from previous generations.

At the lower end of the scale were a smaller number of tenant farmers who moved frequently from one cabin to another in the expectation of getting a better return from a year's work on someone else's land. Between the tenant and the farmer who owned his own land was a class of renters, men who contracted with the landowner to work some of his acreage for a year (or term of years) for which they paid rental either in money or by a share of the crop(s) grown. The route to eventual farm ownership often led through a period of proving to be a "good renter."

The home life of all farm families was closely related to the round of work essential to the production of crops and livestock and upkeep of the farm and homestead. Most farm children grew up learning to assume responsibility for daily chores that had to be carried out in the home or around the farmstead. Farm life in the days of hand tools and animal power required the use of all "hands." Chores that children often helped with included feeding poultry and livestock, milking, getting in wood or coal, hauling out ashes, carrying in water, washing dishes, sweeping, making beds, and various other regular and occasional tasks. And this was but the beginning. Older children, particularly the boys, were required to miss school and help with work on the crops. Many children from tenant families after starting school in July soon had to stop for tobacco cutting. Next came "foddering" and then tobacco stripping, so they just stayed out and got further behind every year. School attendance was viewed by many parents as a matter of secondary priority during seasons of pressing work on the farm or in the family business.

5

Pupils might be sent to school only long enough to learn "to read and write, and figger a little" and then be kept out to work, a practice that played havoc with attendance figures. During the nineteenth century the average attendance never exceeded 40 percent of its potential, which after the Civil War included all children ages 6 through 20.

Despite their heavy regimen of chores, farm children still devised ways to have fun. A most unusual prank by a farm boy was reported by his sister from Wayne County. The boy laid a board across a stump in the barnyard and then shelled corn onto one end. Sundry chickens soon arrived for the feast, whereupon our hero jumped down hard on the other end of the board, sending roosters and hens flying up into the air in somersaults. Naturally this led to some on-the-spot correction by a parental instructor.

But there was little time for recreation, of an approved kind or not. In months of open weather, regular farm work and chores took care of the daylight hours except on Sundays and, in later years, possibly Saturday afternoons. Most families were physically tired after supper and so went to bed early during much of the year. In late fall and winter, farm work ended before an early supper, and after eating, the family gathered around the fireplace or stove, working at odd jobs and entertaining themselves until bedtime. The children usually didn't have a homework assignment to worry about, since most people felt that pupils were long enough at school and had ample study time to "get their lessons" there. Patrons expected the teacher to answer questions pupils might ask, pronounce unfamiliar words, and explain whatever arithmetic problems needed clarification. Few parents were qualified to render much in the way of instructional help, save what could be done with spelling book or multiplication table in hand. Most homes had inadequate facilities for home study in the way of working space, lighting, and the like. Finally, parents and older children were tired after

6

chores were done and supper over, so that homework was not a welcome addition to their tasks.

Children who regularly attended school followed a daily pattern geared to the working day and life-style of the farm family. After the morning chores and breakfast, pupils hastened to get ready for school. This meant changing into school clothes—no great matter since one usually wore the same garb day after day—and getting the "dinner" basket or bucket ready.

The dress of pupils changed gradually through the life of the common school system. In early decades both boys and girls usually wore garments that had been prepared in the home. As cheaper materials became available in the stores, the practice of spinning, weaving, and sewing children's clothes at home declined. Boys tended to wear jeans of homespun fabric to school after most school girls had dresses of store-bought calico. Homemade socks and stockings persisted even longer, especially during the colder months. Few girls had more than two or three dresses—one for school, one for chores and play at home, and one for Sunday. Most started out Monday morning with the school dress freshly starched and clean. Long underwear—red flannels or long handles—had to be worn by both sexes until warm spring weather arrived, and it was heartily disliked by all.

Shoes were an expensive item, especially for families with several children, and were used sparingly in good weather. Nearly all children went to school barefoot until frost in the fall. In the early years shoes were made by traveling cobblers who would board with a family a few days until each person was fitted with a new pair of shoes. Later the cost of shoes at the store caused parents to caution children to save shoe leather. Gum boots were worn by many boys in winter.

In the latter years of the one-teacher schools the girls dressed in ginghams and calicos and wore their hair braided or tied back with ribbons. Boys wore knee-pants with long stockings in winter months. Many remember the old corduroy pants that made a whistling sound when pupils walked. Overalls came into use along with jackets made of the same blue denim material, especially for older boys who wanted to dress like their fathers on the farm. Young fellows felt very important when they could wear a new pair of Carhart overalls with a dollar watch in the pocket made for that purpose on the bib. If a good Barlow knife safely reposed in another pocket a schoolboy was entitled to think of himself as one of no mean status.

Inside the schoolhouse there was not enough individualized instruction to go around, for old-time common schools frequently included pupils who would now be in special education classes. Most former scholars recall schoolmates who "couldn't talk plain," were "hard of hearing," or "couldn't see good." A number of oldtimers remembered pupils who were generally recognized as "weak-minded." Pupils with physical handicaps from "white swelling" or an accident were objects of curiosity for a day or two, and then accepted without question. Another problem for some of the teachers in the early schools was the presence of four-year-olds who were sent to school with older brothers and sisters. Reports tell of teachers who tried to teach them the alphabet and allowed them extra playtime outside during the long days. Some recalled that they were taught their letters while teachers held them on their laps. Not to be forgotten either is the fact that some of the scholars might be twenty years old, often both larger and older than the teacher in charge.

And it was the teacher who was the key to the success of the district schools. The extremely slow and precarious start of the young common school system during the 1840s was partly due to the lack of able teachers who could take charge and show the people what good schools could do.

During the early years the county school commissioners and the district trustees were responsible for

8

examining and certifying persons to teach in the new common schools. Accounts of actual examinations show that this procedure could not be expected to identify many good teachers. An elderly gentleman from Adair County recalled that he had certified many teachers after oral examinations during his several years as an examiner. One applicant found him in the field plowing corn. He smoothed off some plowed ground and had the man write his name with a stick. Next he asked a few questions about arithmetic, reading, history, and geography. Taking the man's word for it that he had studied these subjects, the examiner promised him a certificate and employed him to teach the local school.[1]

At the end of the 1860s two new developments brought about slow but steady improvement of teachers. The first was the introduction of the annual Teachers' Institutes, held in each county of the Commonwealth, and the principal source of instruction for teachers for nearly fifty years. And in 1873 the state superintendent began the practice of preparing and sending to the counties a set of teachers' examination questions for the county examiners should they choose to use them. During the next decade the state board recommended that county examining boards hold written examinations for teachers using the questions furnished by the superintendent, and the practice soon became general.

Aspiring teachers had several ways to prepare for the examinations. Many simply studied at home using school textbooks and a "question book" that provided typical examination questions and answers. Others attended a short-term coaching school or "normal" taught by an experienced teacher, and a few took advantage of the private normal schools established in a number of Kentucky cities in the 1870s and 1880s or of college courses especially planned to prepare teacher candidates. Some applicants who feared to undertake the dreaded two-day ordeal without some advantage followed the illegal, and reprehensible, practice of buying a set of the examination questions from a "questions peddler," an abuse that kept county and state superintendents on edge as long as the examination was required.

Teacher salaries were always low. Though the school term increased from three months to five, six, and then seven months, thus boosting yearly income, the average monthly pay for white and black teachers in the 1900–1901 school year was only $34.10 and $29.95 respectively. Salary disparities among counties and districts were extreme, a condition that continued for many years. But worse than the level of salaries was the fact that teachers did not receive their pay regularly, for often the state's funds were not at hand on time. This situation led to abuses in several counties where orders on the state for salaries due teachers were sometimes sold for ready cash.

Some actual experiences of new teachers tell much about the procedures in the early days. One man from Western Kentucky recalled how he got started:

In October, 1883, I was asked to take a school near Livia, because they could get no one else, and I accepted, because I could get nothing else to do. The law was so poor, and the state had so little money that it was a year before I received my pay.

I taught two months in my first school, before I took the examination, which was oral, conducted by Commissioner Cary and Dr. Haynes, head of the local college in Calhoun. They asked me about twenty questions, and wrote my certificate.[2]

In many neighborhoods teachers had no choice but to board in homes that offered poor accommodations and fare. Some were unsanitary, often food was poorly prepared, and sometimes there were three beds in a room. In one home, the family, schoolteacher, and hired man all had to sleep in the same room. According to the young teacher, it was not so embarrassing to retire at night if the men were all out coon hunting, but the next morning when one awoke with the men present in the room, it was a problem to devise how to get out of bed and dress without the men seeing you. But board was cheap most places—typically $1.50 to $2.00 per week, with the option of staying over for the weekend at no extra charge.

Teachers of the common schools were good representatives of the culture and times that produced them. Or certainly the great majority were. But the general public, especially the patrons and trustees, thought their teachers should be models of behavior and scholarship. This was a large order, especially when teachers were expected to get the needed education, dress well, and live on wages that were not even paid on time. But these same patrons and school officials who had high expectations of their teachers knew from first-hand experience all about low income, hard work, and the need to "try, try again."

The trustees who were responsible for the schools from 1845 to 1934 were not an elite, to be regarded as superior to the rural society they were attempting to serve. Although they were eventually required by state law to be able to read and write, even this qualification was often waived. The school law of 1893 specified a long list of duties and responsibilities, but a great many trustees construed their role as seeing to the upkeep of the schoolhouse and, more important, appointing the teacher. While they were often criticized for favoritism, nepotism, and worse motives in making their decisions, for the most part they probably did the best they could. An old-timer explained how the three-trustee system worked in one community:

How did we satisfy the community? Well, we'd feel around to see how the people felt about the teachers who had applied and when we thought we knew we'd choose. The trustees were elected by popular vote and we wanted to please. . . . Sometimes our elections were hotter than the big election. If they elected a contrary board member we had a time. One man served as chairman, one as clerk. The records were written up and you can see them.

Reports of school elections tend to emphasize the extremes. On the one hand, superintendents complained of lassitude and lack of interest on the part of the patrons, sometimes to the point that elections were not attended and the trustees had to be appointed. At the other extreme there were many reports of bitter controversy, corruption, and violence in connection with school elections. These problems persisted after county school board elections supplanted the trustee elections.

Trustees were supposed to make regular visits to the schools, but apparently this practice gradually declined. One report from the 1880s describes the visits of a trustee, himself illiterate, who always made a speech directed at the boys, never once mentioning the girls. After nearly seventy years, the speech could be recalled almost verbatim:

Now let me tell you little boys—you must study hard and learn as much as you can—learn to read, and write and "figger"— you're shore goin' to need that when you get big and have to tend to your business. I know what I'm talking about—here I am, can't do nothin'—everybody in the county knows more about T—— W——'s business than he does himself. So do as I tell you, study real hard.[3]

The county superintendent also visited the schools. During most of the era this officer was elected by popular vote and incumbents were expected to play the "political game" in their counties. Qualifications for the office were nominal until 1918. It is interesting that women were elected to the office nearly twenty years before they were legally entitled to vote in the local school elections.[4] The county superintendents were expected to visit every district school at least once each year. Pupils were generally instructed to be on their best behavior when the superintendent appeared. Usually this official arrived in a buggy and stayed only a half-hour or so, since most tried to visit three or four schools in a day. Such visits were sometimes pleasant interludes in the school routine. "We were delighted to see him as he would talk to us, tease us, ask questions, have us to tell him our names, and have us to sing." Some teachers made definite preparations for the superintendent's visit. Pupils were warned that they would be questioned about their studies and were urged to be on their best behavior.

In 1908 legislation replaced the district and three-trustee system with one featuring subdistricts, each with a single trustee; the new law added county boards and increased the power of the county superintendent. Criticism was loud and to the point, as we see from this Adair County verse:

> *Three men's opinions are better than one*
> *Except when opinions two have none;*
> *Friends, I do not like the new system for trustee,*
> *Because you can buy one man cheaper than three.*[5]

School leaders were as dissatisfied as the general public with the arrangement, pointing out that county boards and superintendents should have a free hand to select teachers and place them where they would render best service. After various changes in the law during the 1920s and early 1930s, the new school code of 1934 placed all schools under direct control of county boards of education or of independent city boards. The local district trustee became a part of the past.

Poor administrative practices continued even after the county school legislation. Some board members took unto themselves the hiring of teachers and active management of school affairs in their own section of the county. A teacher formerly of Eastern Kentucky recalled that when he returned home from normal school and needed a school, he proposed to visit the county superintendent. His father assured him he didn't have to go see the superintendent. The local board member would take care of it. And so it was settled.

13

Looking back, it is clear that a fundamental shift of policy for the responsibility and control of common schools has occurred since the state undertook to have a statewide system in 1838. Responsibility and control were originally placed in the hands of the people and their elected trustees at the district (grassroots) level. This was what Kentuckians wanted but the responsibility was hard to live up to in most neighborhoods. School districts generally failed to levy local school taxes and continued to look to the meager funds that were distributed from the State School Fund. Through a number of developments the people who wanted local control let the authority be gradually shifted to the state level in the fourth constitution and thereafter. Legislative changes have brought about a division of control between the state and district boards. Today's school districts bear little resemblance to the school "deestrict" of tradition.

Today many Kentuckians are choosing to live in the country, along the blacktop roads that crisscross every county. But most of them are not farmers; they are a new category—"Rural non-farm," according to the Census Bureau. But the changed rural occupancy pattern has not brought back the old-time neighborhood with its mutual assistance, first names, and face-to-face relationships. The new "rurban" areas have come to share some of the same problems that have led to movements in several cities to try out decentralized administration of schools and other services. There was no need for such efforts to bring the schools closer to the people in the heyday of the common schools. While we cannot expect the old-time neighborhood and feelings of local involvement to return like Brigadoon, it would make sense for the schools to stress some of the humane features and values that served people well in the days of the little white schoolhouse.

2

THE LITTLE WHITE SCHOOLHOUSE

ANYONE WHO HAS read Whittier's verses about the schoolhouse sunning by the road like a ragged beggar would agree that the description fitted most of Kentucky's common schools during much of their history. After the log schools were replaced by frame buildings and the hewn-log furniture by dressed poplar fixtures, the physical environment remained unchanged for many decades. Outside, the trees grew taller and thicker, playgrounds eroded, and the public road wore down between banks that became steeper, but these changes took place gradually and were hardly noticed. The little white schoolhouse was part of the typical Kentucky rural scene for five or six decades. A good number remain even today, but almost all have long since been converted to dwellings or put to other uses by the growing population.

One of the many problems that plagued the school leaders through the years was that of getting several thousands of school districts to build adequate and comfortable schoolhouses. The log-cabin structures that had been built by the pioneer settlers gradually deteriorated until they were not only inadequate but also hazardous. Superintendents chided trustees and commissioners for failing to get voters in the districts to tax themselves for the purpose of building safe and decent schoolhouses. Frequently the school reports and newspapers charged that Kentucky's farmers provided better shelter for their livestock than for their children.

One of Superintendent H. A. M. Henderson's chief concerns in the reestablishment of schools following the Civil War was the improvement of school buildings. Since it was generally acknowledged that good schools required good schoolhouses, he urged parents to demand adequate buildings. The comfort and health of the children required sturdy, well-lighted, warm, and easily ventilated school buildings. Instead, they were housed in buildings characterized by forbidding appearance, inadequate space, and poor ventilation. Furthermore, there was insufficient playground space, and no outbuildings were provided. The average schoolhouse was described as "a little square, squatty, unhewed log building, blazing in the sun, standing upon the dusty highway or some bleak and barren spot that has been robbed of every tree and blossoming shrub, without yard, fence, or other surrounding suggestive of comfort to abate its bare, cold, hard, and hateful look."[1] Such surroundings could have only negative effects on students' efforts to learn their lessons. School officials and parents were urged to institute reforms at once by replacing the old buildings with convenient comfortable schoolhouses.

Henderson's strong language and ambitious plans for schoolhouses were largely ignored. Few people saw the need to get excited about the little schoolhouse which was used mostly in summer and fall months and which had many of the same features, good and bad, as their own houses and farm buildings. Over the years state superintendents were to reiterate many of the complaints and admonitions about common schoolhouses before the situation was substantially improved.

Before 1908, schoolhouses could be financed by one of three plans: trustees of a district could levy a tax of $0.25 per $100 of taxable property; voters of a district could levy a poll tax of $2.00 upon each male twenty years of age and older; or the people of a district could build a school themselves by furnishing the materials and labor. The last was the most commonly used method in the early decades. Despite the urgings of superintendents and continued criticism in the press, many district trustees were unwilling to levy local taxes and few citizens chose to vote a poll tax upon themselves. The 1894 school law (an addition to the comprehensive act of 1893) provided that trustees might be prosecuted and fined if they failed to provide a suitable schoolhouse within a year's time. Standards for schoolhouses included a total value of house, grounds, furnishings, and equipment of not less than $150; space of not less than ten square feet for each child of school age in the district; minimum height of ten feet from floor to ceiling; a minimum of four windows; one or more fireplaces with safe flues; and one or more doors with locks and keys to be held by the chairman of the district board of trustees, who was responsible for property damage due to neglect. These provisions were not met in the Commonwealth.

There was, however, gradual improvement over the years in types of district schoolhouses. During the two decades of 1881–1901, the number of log schoolhouses declined from 3,360 to 1,238; simultaneously, the number of frame buildings increased from 2,138 to 6,752; and brick structures increased slightly from 145 to 150.[2] Concern about the type and quality of schoolhouses continued to arouse discussion in the first decade of the 1900s. The Kentucky Federation of Women's Clubs, the Louisville Commercial Club, and other groups supported studies of schoolhouses and grounds with a view to agreement upon a model that could be adopted widely across the state.

In this period, considerable interest was expressed in the matter of school sites which could be improved by landscaping and which would afford adequate space for playgrounds and school gardens. Many people saw the need for country schools to provide instruction in agriculture, horticulture, conservation, domestic science, manual arts, and other practical fields of study. Various leaders and groups studied school developments in neighboring states, and this accelerated public interest in school consolidation. Looking back, Kentucky educators may well ponder the question of why the rural schools, bound as they were to the agrarian way of life, failed to teach agriculture, homemaking, beautification of grounds, and the like. Why should it have been necessary to close schools near to farm homes and haul children to consolidated centers to provide this kind of curriculum enrichment and other advantages?

Early in the post–World War I period noteworthy studies of Kentucky education were made by the Kentucky Educational Commission (1921) and the Efficiency Commission of Kentucky (1923).[3] The first of these, undertaken with the assistance of the General Education Board, was considered an objective review of the educational status of the Commonwealth. The situation may be visualized from the following excerpts from the report:

Approximately 50 percent of these schoolhouses are painted and in good repair. . . . The other half in most instances never had even an initial coat of paint, and are in ill repair. The roofs leak, the weather boarding is off here and there; doors are broken, knobs gone, window panes out, walls stained, floors uneven and cracked, seats broken and out of place, and a pall of dust over all. These neglected schoolhouses teach eloquently the doctrine of shiftlessness, disorder and indifference. . . . An upright Burnside stove furnishes heat, the fire being started by the first person who reaches school, whether pupil or teacher. . . . The stove usually stands in the center or front center of the room. . . . A galvanized bucket with the common drinking cup almost invariably takes the place of a sanitary drinking fountain; lavatory facilities are non-existent. The blackboard usually consists of a front wall and a few side walls painted black. . . . In a few counties, each school has in addition to the above equipment, a globe, maps of the world,

18

of the United States, and of Kentucky, and a number of charts for reading, physiology, etc. . . . . Rural teachers are their own janitors. . . . . About half of the rural schools have wells or cisterns; at the other half, water is carried from a nearby spring or well. In the mountain counties toilets are practically unknown. . . . . Rural school grounds are invariably small. . . . . Besides these one-room rural buildings, there are one or more two-, three-, and even four-room schoolhouses in almost every county of the state.[4]

The report also depicted the state of school buildings in smaller graded school districts and even 40 percent of city schools. It recommended that consolidated schools replace one-room schools wherever road conditions permitted. It was assumed that it would always be necessary to maintain one-room schools in a number of Knobs counties and in the mountains. But even there, "the present shacks should be replaced as rapidly as possible by modern structures, well lighted, heated, and ventilated, with a classroom, cloakrooms, a small room for cooking, another small room for agriculture and manual training, and sanitary lavatory and toilet facilities. Outside there should be a well, coal shed, and a horse shed."[5] Further recommendations called for rural school grounds to be enlarged and improved with ample space for free play and agricultural demonstration plots.

The commission's study of schoolhouses may be summed up in this quotation: "The schoolhouse situation is thus extremely bad. Surely education in cleanliness, orderliness, respect for property, modesty, physical well-being, and hygienic living is an essential part of the school's task; yet the great majority of the children of the state, both white and colored, are housed year after year in structures that themselves violate every maxim that education should directly and indirectly impress upon the child."[6] It was estimated that the financial loss to the state through poor schoolhouse planning and construction had been upwards of $10 million during the first two decades of the twentieth century.

19

No action was taken. Recommended improvements presented a price tag that appeared far beyond the resources of the taxpayers, not to mention the courage of the school boards to levy taxes. It was easier for many people to ignore the findings of the commission. Efforts of most educational leaders were devoted to consolidation and the construction of new public high schools. As these efforts proved successful, the new schools would replace the little one-teacher schools. When the Efficiency Commission of Kentucky made its report on education in 1923, there was little discussion of the problems of the state's schoolhouses and facilities.

Relatively little improvement in the state's schoolhouses was effected in the 1920s. The Kentucky Educational Commission report of 1933 presented the following findings: (1) Eighty-two percent of elementary school children in county districts still attended small (one-, two-, and three-teacher) schools, the majority of which were of frame construction, poorly planned, and located on inadequate sites; (2) schoolhouses of county districts included 22 percent erected before 1907 that should be abandoned; (3) rural school sites were invariably too small, lacking adequate usable playing space and playground equipment.[7] It appeared that the state's one-teacher schools, after a quarter-century under the county school law, were housed in substantially the same kind of facilities that had served the parents of the pupils.

Recollections of many former common school scholars provide glimpses inside old-time school rooms. Uncomfortable, crowded, smelly, unsightly, isolated though they may have been, none of it sounds forbidding and unendurable when recounted by those who learned in those same surroundings. An old-timer remembered the puncheon floor of the old Sugar Creek schoolhouse in Garrard County where he started to school in the 1870s. The furniture consisted of primitive long wooden benches for the pupils. An open fireplace consumed great logs, but most of the heat went up the chimney. Water was carried from a nearby spring and was drunk from a common gourd dipper. Part of the year the schoolhouse door stood open and occasionally livestock would use the building for shelter in bad weather.

A fairly typical picture of the schools most children attended in the early part of this century is presented by the Irish Bottom school in Cumberland County. It was a frame building with one door at the front, facing the road, three windows on each side, and a painted blackboard across the back end. Double desks, graduated in size, accommodated the pupils. Boys and girls were seated on opposite sides of the room, according to custom in all common schools until well into this century. Two long recitation benches faced the teacher's desk and blackboard. A rectangular cast-iron stove, with two eyes that could be slanted sideways to emit heat, stood in the center. It burned wood with an insatiable appetite in cold weather. In winter months, attendance invariably fell off, and then the recitation benches were placed on either side of the stove. By 1910 the ubiquitous water bucket that sat on a shelf or bench by the front door was replaced with a water cooler, and individual folding metal cups took the place of the old common dipper. A well was drilled near the school in 1912. The surrounding playground had six large beech trees for shade.

In earlier years school housekeeping was a shared responsibility. Older scholars were expected to keep the wood fire going in the huge fireplace, haul water from the nearest spring or fresh stream, and sweep the floor. Building fires was the teacher's responsibility, which meant getting an early start in the mornings. In later years, many teachers arranged for an older boy to come early to fire up and get the room warm before the pupils arrived—usually at a rate of twenty-five cents a week. The task was made easier when the tall, coal-burning pot-bellied stoves came into use. Bringing in fuel from the coalhouses and carrying out ashes were the major tasks for the remainder of common school days.

Equipment in the old-time common school was strictly limited. Furniture was homemade until around the turn of the century, and teaching equipment was left to the inventiveness of the teacher and pupils. For most rural schools early in this century, equipment generally included chalk and erasers for blackboard, chart for beginners (ABCs and numerals, etc.), dictionary (possibly on a stand), globe, library books, map of Kentucky, world map, oil lamps on brackets, pictures of Washington and Lincoln, and window shades.

Most of these materials were purchased with money raised by box or pie suppers. Library books, when available, were borrowed by pupils and read at home by several members of the family. In neighborhoods that maintained exceptional interest in their schools, there might be financial assistance in providing some such amenity as window curtains. Window screens and screen doors were luxury items and unknown until recent years. After the county boards became responsible for all rural common schools in 1908, the tax revenue of the county and expenditures for furniture and equipment increased gradually, but for decades there were grave disparities among the counties in the funds available.

Outside the little schoolhouse, the playground space and the toilet facilities left much to be desired. Such space was not considered in the early years when sites for schoolhouses were usually donated by landowners. Donors did not offer their best acreage, nor did they select level space for play and recreation. Most parents were not concerned with promoting play, and what play there was could be adapted to the available space and facilities. This philosophy prevailed for most of the years of the common schools in Kentucky. The saving feature in this seemingly stark picture is that resilient, adaptable youth, given the chance, proved able to provide their own entertainment. Schoolgrounds, without facilities and space for elaborate games, were occupied at recess and dinner hours with active participants in play activities of a wide variety.

Common school pupils often had to meet personal needs without provision of facilities. Pupils went by common agreement into the woods or thickets (even the cliffs in a few instances) to answer calls of nature. Even after outside facilities were provided, they were generally in unsatisfactory condition much of the time. Little was done to improve the unpleasant features, save an occasional application of lime which was effective for only a brief period. The problem of unauthorized inscriptions and lifelike drawings on the walls of the outbuildings plagued teachers and parents, but the day of the common school waned and passed with no solution. Testimony from some reminiscences indicates that terms and anatomical details seen on the walls contributed to a learning experience not offered by well-worn textbooks.

Health precautions taken in the several homes neither prevented disease nor added to the attractiveness of the school environment. No one who experienced the redolent atmosphere of the packed schoolroom in bad weather will have difficulty in recalling the many smells that could be identified: coal smoke—sulfurous fumes from low-grade fuel; drying outergarments, stockings, and shoes; homespun poultices featuring turpentine and lard on flannel rags. All these met, mingled, and competed for olfactory attention until overpowered by the clear-cut winner—the amulets of asafetida worn by sundry scholars to ward off contagion. Mere words do not suffice to recapture the pervasive nature of these stimuli to the sense organs.

Lice were also a problem inherent in these conditions. Outbreaks of these minute but not-to-be-ignored invaders were fairly common in old-time schools much to the chagrin of status-conscious parents and the discomfiture of their offspring. Sometimes an entire school would be infested. Another contagious condition that disturbed conscientious mothers even more was the "itch." The common home remedy carried the unmistakable odor of sulfur which told its own tale.

Most services that later came to be expected from county health departments were not provided in rural schools until the one-teacher schools were already on their way out. Reports of early visits by county health nurses who "came round to vaccinate and give shots" began in the 1920s. By the time public health departments got programs well under way, the majority of the state's children were in consolidated and urban schools. Traditional attitudes and viewpoints toward health and sanitation measures changed slowly even among persons whose educational achievement was above average. A member of the Henderson City Council, himself a doctor, disapproved of medical inspection of children in public schools. "I was raised in a mud-daubed schoolhouse in the country, where you could stick your fingers in the mud between the logs, and we all drank out of the same drinking cup, and there was not a healthier set anywhere than that bunch of children, and we didn't have any sterilized rags to wipe the dust off of sterilized desks. The doctors are all but crazy."[8]

Many old-time scholars recall their common school days with genuine pleasure despite conditions and experiences that would now be considered rough:

Thinking back now we really had a wonderful time going to school in those days. We would all get to school early and play in the school yard. At 7:00 Mr. Wilson would ring the hand bell and we would all run into the school room. And he would start right out with the 1st reader up in front of the class reading out loud and the rest of us would study. I remember that Mr. Wilson used to make me stand on one foot and write right-handed because he would catch me using my left hand. He almost ruined me and I can say right now he treated us like a bunch of dogs. During lunch period we would play under the big shade trees and have a wonderful time. In the afternoon we would have writing and arithmetic and the boys in the class were always pulling tricks on Mr. Wilson, they would steal his switches, put dirt in the water, and when the boys' dogs would follow them to school they would bring them in the classroom and they would lay by the benches until school was out. I enjoyed the trip home best of all because we would play in the road building castles and picking our lunch baskets full of berries.

A later reminiscence told of school days under less strenuous conditions:

The one-room school as I remember was far from tiresome or boring. I found it very entertaining and also very learningful to follow the lessons of the classes that were under and above my grade. I think this helped to keep the schoolroom quiet and orderly. I found this part of school very fascinating.

All the children knew one another and their families. You felt closer to one another, their troubles were your troubles. You learned sympathy for the more unfortunate students and their families. Clothes were shared or given to the poor.

Former teachers of common schools stressed some of the same advantages and strengths. One who attended and later taught one-room schools offered a balanced view: "I liked the individuality of the one-room school and I believe its best features are on the way back. My most serious criticism of the old common school is that teachers and pupils could not do justice to so many subjects that had to be taught in even the longer school day."

Not every old-time scholar liked the common schools. Occasionally one expressed strong negative feelings: "I didn't like anything about the old-time common school. I just knew I had to go. I didn't know there was such a thing as a high school. The thing that I disliked most was the daily six-mile walk. I lived for the day to quit school and start farming." The same man expressed distaste for certain subjects, especially geography. Others disliked arithmetic and grammar because they could not see their

25

usefulness. On the other hand, some teachers used various methods to make arithmetic meaningful and challenging by posing practical problems to be solved. Achieving relevancy is a common problem in schools.

Many pupils liked and respected a teacher or teachers and this was reason enough to like school. Memories that are most often recalled and recounted tend to involve personal relationships. Little triumphs of the spelling bees and ciphering matches were treasured memories by persons who have had other more spectacular successes as adults, but the latter are seldom recounted with such satisfaction. Some pupils were able to lay a solid educational foundation in the common school that offered a start into professional study. Many speak of the joys of being together with children of neighbors and with kinfolks and of good times they had in the little white school. And many preferred school to the alternative of work.

The little white schoolhouse is gone. But with all its shortcomings and inadequacies it was accepted as a matter of fact by thousands of pupils, many of whom came from houses that had some of the same features and problems.

3

DEAR OLD
GOLDEN RULE DAYS

THE DAILY WALK to and from school provided many children with the few opportunities they had to be free from the supervision of parents and teachers. It was not uncommon for children to walk five or more miles each day, over all kinds of roads and trails, through woods and fields. Many hazards were encountered—creeks to cross, hills to climb, mean dogs, angry ganders, snakes, stray animals, mud in winter and dust in summer, heat and cold, rain and winds. If the route led through pasture fields there were bulls, butting sheep, billy goats, or other beasts to avoid. Nearly every year rural neighborhoods had mad dog scares, and children would be warned to climb the nearest fence or tree if they saw a dog staggering or frothing at the mouth. Another occasional hazard was the appearance of a caravan of gypsy wagons. Parents cautioned children to stay together, to hurry straight home, even to hide if they saw gypsies coming, for "they kidnap children." Other dangers sometimes mentioned were tramps, especially in districts with railroad trackage, and chance meetings with wandering "crazy people." As the days grew perceptibly shorter in the fall and winter, children who lived farthest from school often reached home after dark, which tended to increase the hazards of their daily walks.

Many children found it necessary to cross a creek or branch on their way to school. This might mean stepping carefully on strategically placed stones to avoid getting wet, but even this arrangement was useless when the creek flooded after heavy rains. Some neighborhoods, especially in mountain counties, constructed swinging footbridges across major streams, but it was often necessary to walk greater distances to make use of such improvements. A common provision for crossing a creek was the footlog, which called for sure footing, steady nerves, and a certain degree of daring. A slip of the foot, an attack of dizziness, or a little push by some mischievous classmate usually meant a good wetting and a scolding at home. Most pupils, however, rushed through the hazards of their walk (which they hardly noticed) to reach school early, both because teachers disapproved of tardiness and because this allowed some playtime.

At eight o'clock the bell sounded for "books." The bell may have been mounted on a pole or hung in a belfry. Before bells were in common use, teachers might rap on the wall or call the children together. After the seating came the roll call, to which the scholars answered "present." Often pupils would explain the absences of other children. Some teachers opened the school day with exercises, chiefly devotional in nature; a brief scripture reading, possibly the Lord's Prayer repeated in unison, followed by "My Country 'Tis of Thee" or another song or hymn was a typical pattern. A few teachers asked the pupils to respond to the roll by reciting a verse of scripture or a quotation. In the twentieth century the "Pledge of Allegiance" became a fixture in opening exercises.

Next came the first round of recitations, beginning with the primer class and followed by the classes in readers, from first through fifth. In the early years recitations were individualized as teacher and pupil followed the book together. Beginners in reading started by memorizing the alphabet, usually with the aid of a chart; then, using the phonetic approach, they learned to recognize and pronounce words. The school days were long, and sometimes teachers allowed the youngest children to take naps at their desks or to play outside extra time to break the long schedule.

In the earliest schools scholars stood for recitations. In later years the long recitation benches became standard equipment. When more subjects were added and classes became larger, teachers introduced more tightly controlled daily schedules, and class recitations replaced much of the individualized instruction.

In the earliest years, pupils learned mostly by oral memorization; the result was a veritable babel of sound. Old-timers have often explained the "blab school" as necessary because this was the only way the schoolmaster knew that the pupils were busy. This procedure was discontinued during the 1870s, when Superintendent Henderson urged the teachers to organize their classes by means of a schedule of recitations. Before 1870 common schools were composed of two divisions, primary and elementary. In the 1870s this scheme was revised to provide three divisions, primary, intermediate, and advanced, with pupils divided according to the reader they were using. This loose form of organization continued until the Department of Education recommended organization of common schools on the eight-grades plan in the 1890s, a reorganization that was not completed until well into the twentieth century.

In the years before the development of a more extensive curriculum, the younger children read or "recited" up to four times daily. When there were large numbers of beginners, teachers asked certain advanced scholars to help with the instruction. As pupils moved into the primer and the several readers, instruction in numbers and spelling began.

Arithmetic usually followed reading in the daily

schedule. In most early schools these two subjects filled the time before recess. Only fifteen minutes long and religiously observed by most teachers, recess provided welcome relief from the long inactivity of sitting on hard benches and trying to give attention to the same old textbooks over and over. It was a chance, too, to chomp on an apple kept in one's pocket or to open the dinner bucket for a gingersnap or tea cake to hold one's appetite in check until lunchtime. But mostly, recess was for play.

After the hurried burst of play, the children returned to the waiting books. Only one or two needs might delay a prompt return to the morning school work. One need involved a rather lengthy period of time at the outdoor facilities, and the other was for time to quench one's thirst. The teacher frequently asked two older boys to pass the water bucket to each row of children in turn. It was considered good manners to dip out no more water than one could drink, but if some did happen to be left in the dipper, it was sprinkled on the floor. Sometimes little urchins drank from the gourd dipper two or three times before they were satisfied. In such cases, there could be little surprise if the sounds of belching were later heard.

After arithmetic came various recitations, and then came spelling. Pupils spelled in groups according to the reader they were using. Standing in a straight line facing the teacher, they spelled words orally. Written recitations in spelling were not common until well into the twentieth century.

By noon everyone was ready for dinner. Generally, getting one's lunch and finding a suitable place to eat was a hurried, no-nonsense business. Children of the same family would gather around the eldest member who portioned out the contents of the basket or pail. During good weather everyone ate outdoors, sitting under the shade trees which, despite Superintendent Henderson's report, flourished on most school grounds. Sometimes in the rush to get outside and claim a favorite eating place, a child would trip and fall, dinner and all. Such a misfortune might bring forth some donations, but generally the loser had to salvage whatever he could. Such experiences taught the old admonition about "making haste slowly" more effectively than the wise instructions of the teacher.

As the children seated themselves and laid out their dinners, they were often joined by a passel of dogs of diverse descriptions. Roused from their snooze under the schoolhouse by the dinner exit, the four-footed friends came forth to share in the feast. Often the pickings were slim, and dogfights ensued. But much of the time there were chicken bones, fat meat scraps, pieces of bread, cake crumbs, piecrust, and the like to be snapped for when thrown into the dirt by the diners. Anything the dogs disdained was picked up and discarded.

Size of the dinner basket varied with the number of children in a family. A half-gallon tin bucket sufficed for a single child, while two-gallon buckets were needed for larger families. The fare depended upon the season and to some extent upon the culinary expertise of the cook at home. Typical summer lunches of children from substantial farm homes often included ham or fried chicken, biscuits with jelly or jam, fresh tomatoes, corn on the cob, baked sweet potato, and pie or cake. Later in the fall after "hog killin' time," the meat was spare ribs or sausage, with fried potato cakes or baked sweet potato, sorghum molasses, biscuits with jam, jelly, or marmalade, milk in a bottle, and fried fruit pie. Fried and boiled eggs were common, as was corn bread, and sometimes there were tea cakes. Dinner pails of children from homes of tenant farmers and the poor were not filled as heavily nor with such variety. Corn bread, sowbelly, rabbit, and coarser fare were common. In general, the scholar's fare was more of what was had at home modified chiefly by the practicability of packing it so that the "vittles" would survive handling until they were eaten. This meant food that was in season or that had been canned, cured, dried, smoked, preserved, or stored for use after the growing season. Provident mothers tried to include canned tomatoes, fruits, and other vegetables in the dinner pails, but the hazards of spills often resulted in a messy lunchtime.

Two firsthand accounts relate the happy experiences of the dinner hour:

There were about four or five in my family going to school. We carried our dinner in a big old willow basket that had been made. We took fried potatoes, biscuits, cornbread, a molasses can filled with milk, and sack full of apples we had picked. If Ma happened to cook soup beans we'd take some of them. There weren't no need in tradin' cause just about everybody had the same thing. We'd eat and then spread the scraps over the yard. If we still had time we'd play some games before we'd go back in.

Everyone carried his lunch to school, usually in a metal molasses bucket with a tight lid to keep the ants out. For lunch cold meat sandwiches (sausage, tenderloin, ham, bacon), egg sandwiches, cake, and an apple in season; also home-made cookies, and bread and jelly (or preserves) sandwiches. In pretty weather [they] ate outside and in bad weather they would have to stay inside to eat. They did not usually trade food as parents warned them not to do it. A dog from the nearest farmhouse was usually there at lunch-time to eat the scraps.

Occasionally children were subjected to disparaging remarks about their dinners or manner of eating. Some stories of such incidents have what might be termed a happy ending. A retired railroad conductor recalled how he handled a smart aleck who criticized the dinner brought by his brothers and sisters and their manner of eating, each with his or her own spoon carried in a pocket. Since he was the eldest boy, he picked up a round stone about the size of a duck egg and threw it, striking the fellow in the middle of the forehead and opening a bloody cut. The incident was reported to the teacher and the boy was severely whipped, but there were no more remarks about the N—— children and their eating habits.

In good weather, the outside diners usually hurried through their meals in order to have maximum time for play. Cold and inclement weather, which usually meant eating at one's desk, resulted in somewhat more leisurely dining habits, although even cold weather could not deter some of the hardiest scholars who would eat standing outside. Inside, scraps were usually fed into the pot-bellied stove which was not selective about its fuel requirements. Use of napkins was extremely rare until paper napkins became common. Few school dinners included utensils other than spoons for dishes of liquid content. Dinner at the old-time common school, like most meals at the homes of the scholars, was a simple affair, albeit an enjoyable respite from the rigorous morning schedule.

Teachers ate either at their desks or, in good weather, in a shady, comfortable spot. On those occasions when the teacher had spent the night at the home of a patron, the children of that family and the teacher would share the dinner prepared by the hostess. Sometimes the housewife would try to "put the big pot into the little one" and provide a fancy lunch. This might mean inclusion of knives, forks, and linen napkins. The degree of enjoyment of such repasts depended upon the relationships between teachers and pupils involved, as many former scholars have recalled those days.

Skylarking and humor were a normal part of the dinner hour. Often someone would offer to trade some item from his menu for something more to his taste. The bargaining and banter that accompanied the deal sometimes offered a junior-sized preview of the bartering that took place on Court Day. As soon as someone finished eating the "boy-piece" of chicken, there would be a wishbone-pulling contest.

Teasing took place during the dinner hour, as it did at

various other points during the school day, the amount and variety of it depending upon teacher supervision and opportunity for other recreation. Even during "books" teasing could be done by means of grimaces, naughty gestures, lip movements, and winking. A pupil could express derision of another by a whittling motion of one index finger over the other or by mouthing the words "shamey, shamey" without sound. One common form of teasing in the school yard was to make fun of anything unusual in the dress or appearance of another pupil. Children of families that could not afford adequate clothing and other necessities often carried hurt from "funmaking" by thoughtless schoolmates. Boys teased girls for being fat, scrawny, or red-headed, and pulled their plaits or curls. Younger pupils were teased for poor coordination and lack of athletic ability. Teenage pupils teased each other about sweethearts.

Sometimes an accident or mishap brought about teasing of the victim. Such was the case recalled by a former scholar who became a teacher of common schools: "Teasing was carried on all the time. I recall one instance when a boy fell into one of the many cowpiles that were in the school yard. He had to be taken to the creek and he and his clothes washed. We teased him about that for a long time."

Though most teachers and pupils remained at school during the noon hour, pupils from nearby farms were permitted to go home for their dinner. A few teachers lived close enough to do the same, but this involved some risks. One of the most interesting stories of what did happen when the teacher was absent at dinner time came from Johnson County in the 1930s. On this particular day the health nurse had visited the school to administer smallpox vaccinations. As she finished she threw the cotton and used needles in the wastebasket by the teacher's desk. Unsupervised during the dinner hour, the pupils decided to play "nurse." Several students were duly "vaccinated" again with the discarded needles.

Shortly thereafter, a number of pupils showed up with two sore arms and later boasted more than one vaccination scar.

At one o'clock the bell summoned everyone back to books. The youngest children were called up for their letters or to read again. Geography and history for primary and advanced students followed before the midafternoon recess.

After recess the beginners and the primary department pupils recited again. Two classes for primary and advanced physiology usually were held at this time. Finally, toward the end of the day the advanced pupils recited in their civil government class. By four o'clock everyone was ready to go home, and school usually dismissed at that time.

Coats and wraps were gathered up, dinner baskets and buckets collected, farewells called, and the scholars left for home. Sometimes certain pupils remained in school after dismissal time, not by choice but for disciplinary purposes. Scholars might voluntarily remain after school to get extra help from the teacher, but this was relatively rare.

The long school day ended, the children went storming forth to freedom. Some played last lick or tag with schoolmates until the paths toward home separated. Those who dared to dawdle along the way found diverse excuses for dalliance. Orchards and melon patches were temptations for some of the older boys; the streams with crawdads, "minners," and frogs always proved interesting; on hot summer afternoons the old swimming hole inspired many to ignore the matin warning to "come straight home"; siblings who would go home and tell tales out of school had to be cajoled and dealt with; rocks waited to be skipped across ponds and pools; "grape trees" that hung with ripening "possum" and fox grapes needed climbing; autumnal fruits like pawpaws and persimmons were distractions; and a host of inviting prospects were open to investigation by sharp young lads. The girls shared in many extracurricular activities. They gathered chestnuts, hazel nuts, hickory nuts, and walnuts, shared apples and pears that hung invitingly over the fence rows and roads, and chatted with their schoolmates. Younger pupils, both boys and girls, tended to stick together, particularly when older brothers and sisters disliked being bothered with them, preferring the company of their peers in age and interests.

Some children amused themselves on the long walks to and from school by daring each other to perform feats such as walking along the top of the fence, walking the rails on the railroad, or sneaking into a farmer's orchard. Throwing rocks at anything along the road was almost a daily ritual; fence posts, tree trunks, songbirds, and those beautiful brown or green insulators on the telegraph poles alongside the railroad tracks were handy targets.

Another form of amusement was to engage in rock fights with fellow students or outsiders. In winter, snowballs provided an ample supply of ammunition for many contests of skill and dodging. Pupils from an old-time school in Fayette County frequently engaged in rock and snowball fights with children from a neighboring black school. At one point their routes crossed a creek and here the battle would be joined, with the opponents throwing at each other from opposite banks of the stream. Deciding that this was becoming a serious matter, the teachers arranged changes in their daily schedules so that dismissal times were different, and the battles ceased.

Often some of the older pupils had disagreements, and controversy broke out on the way home from school. Fights resulted, sometimes with serious consequences. Teachers usually whipped participants the next day at school. Sometimes pupils who were determined to fight over their differences would go home first, and then meet to do battle when they were no longer under the teacher's discipline.

Despite the distances and hazards encountered, most scholars appeared to enjoy their walks to and from school and interesting stories have been recounted concerning these experiences. Hazards encountered on these trips were sometimes unusual:

My two older brothers and I were walking home through a pasture that ended in a high cliff that overhung a creek. A ram chased us so Sam and I climbed out on an old crooked tree growing over the cliff. The ram followed us out on the tree and were we scared! Fortunately, our older brother, Will, who had not climbed out on the tree came and pushed the ram off the tree. He rolled twenty or thirty feet down the cliff.

But after all the adventures of the day, the pupils finally reached home—and the evening chores in store for them there.

4

READIN', 'RITIN', AND 'RITHMETIC

For a great number of people over the years the old-time common school has been described in the nostalgic words of the popular song of yesteryear: "Readin' and 'ritin' and 'rithmetic, / Taught to the tune of a hickory stick." There was a little more to the curriculum, but not much more. For Kentucky common schools in the early years, the curriculum was defined by law as including the so-called common branches, a term that distinguished the fundamental subjects from those that belonged to the secondary or collegiate levels (algebra, Latin, modern languages, etc.). The common branches were well defined by custom and traditions of the schools that preceded the common school system. By an act of 1852, the General Assembly specified what could be taught: "The instruction prescribed by the board [state board of education] shall not go beyond the elements of a plain education in English, including grammar, arithmetic, and geography." This was popularly interpreted to mean what were called the 3 Rs, along with spelling (orthography), English grammar, and geography. This legislative action was taken against the wishes of Superintendent Robert J. Breckinridge, who wanted the legislature to broaden the course of study: "A course of good common school instruction should contemplate a thorough knowledge of spelling, reading, writing, geography, with maps, arithmetic, the history of the United States, English Grammar, in all its elementary principles, including composition, and the elements of general history."[1] In his recommendations the superintendent was supported by the findings of a convention of "The Friends of Public Education in Kentucky," which he called in November 1851 to review basic questions about the common schools and to advise on policy. The minimum course of study prescribed by the General Assembly shaped the common school offerings for future decades.

From time to time the legislature added subjects to the common branches:

1864—United States history
1884—English composition; laws of health
1888—elements of civil government; physiology and hygiene to replace laws of health
1893—history of Kentucky
1918—annual observance of Temperance Day; elementary agriculture
1920—physical training and thrift
1922—singing
1924—daily Bible reading required; United States Constitution
1928—public speaking, discussion, debating, and parliamentary law

The influence of certain pressure groups is clearly evident in the legislation, but the effect upon instruction was not impressive. The normal schools (soon to be teachers' colleges) instituted courses for students seeking teachers' certificates, but there is grave doubt that the new courses and requirements received attention in the one-room schools comparable to that accorded to the traditional common branches. Neither the time nor the preparation of the teachers appeared adequate.

The principal tools for both teachers and scholars in the

common schools were the textbooks. In most schools the books studied and pored over constituted the curriculum. What came out of the hours of study and recitation was what was conveyed by William Holmes McGuffey, Noah Webster, Joseph Ray, Noble Butler, or other authors of popular textbooks. Since the education based on these limited sources proved quite successful, it suggests that the rural agrarian culture, the little white schoolhouse, the schoolmasters as local products of these institutions, most patrons, and the language and values of the textbooks put together by articulate spokesmen of that same culture all supported and reinforced one another.

Scholars from the earlier decades of the common school almost to a person expressed strong feelings of approval and appreciation for the books they studied. Few other kinds of reading matter were available to the great majority of pupils at home; school libraries were practically nonexistent until a few districts assembled small collections after the turn of the century. Few newspapers and magazines came to most homes. The nearest thing to the radio or television set or even the phonograph was the party telephone line that linked some of the more affluent farm families with the nearest towns, and this came late in the nineteenth century or even later. Clearly, the books read by youthful scholars had something approaching a monopoly on the ideas and values that would be considered, verbalized, and possibly acted upon.

It is perhaps well that the scholars who used the treasured school books did not know some of the difficulties their political and educational leaders were having in finding the right procedure for selecting and providing the textbooks. For many decades this was one of the thorniest and most persistent problems to plague the schools and people of the Commonwealth.

In the early years of the common schools, the pupils used whatever books their parents could provide. Instruction was principally on an individual basis and the teachers did their best to assist the pupils in mastering the material in the books at hand. The school law in 1844 explicitly acknowledged the right and responsibility of parents to decide upon textbooks. Acting counter to the advice of Breckinridge, the legislature in 1852 changed this policy and authorized the state board to recommend textbooks that would be purchased by parents for use by their children at school. This arrangement continued for some twenty years despite complaints about changes that required parents to spend hard-to-get money for new books. Changes of the law in 1884, 1888, and 1893 failed to satisfy anyone concerned, although three different plans were tried. The law authorized the state board to recommend lists of suitable books from which trustees of the several districts should adopt books for their schools. These adoptions were not to change more often than every five years. This policy resulted in much diversity among books used in districts of even the same counties and produced cries for uniformity to save parents money. The uproar was aided and abetted by certain book companies that sought to gain a virtual monopoly in the Commonwealth. From this time forward, there were more frequent changes in the textbook laws, and even more frequent efforts to change them in every session of the General Assembly. The book companies of Louisville and Cincinnati engaged in strong competition for some time, but the eventual winner for a considerable period was the American Book Company. This strong organization was formed by a merger of smaller publishers that had provided some of the most popular textbooks.

In 1904 the first state Textbook Commission was established and given power to adopt a state list from those submitted by the 119 county commissioners. This arrangement lasted until 1910, when county commissioners took over the responsibility. In 1914 the Textbook Commission was reinstated, with twelve members appointed by the governor. City school systems made their own adoptions, but county schools and schools of the smaller towns had to use the state list. A scandal in 1919

41

resulted in a court case and the adoption of a new list by the Textbook Commission. After many complicated actions and repercussions, often politically motivated, the textbook problem was highlighted in the 1925 legislative campaign. The 1926 General Assembly passed laws creating a new state Textbook Commission and required a uniform adoption for the whole state. The issue of free textbooks was interjected into the 1927 gubernatorial campaign. The 1928 legislature enacted a law to make this provision, but no funds were made available until the legislative session of 1934. In 1930 the legislature reconstituted the state Textbook Commission, to be composed of educators and to be independent of the governor's control. The commission adopted a basic list of books for county and small-city systems and a multiple list from which cities of the first four classes would make their own selections. Adoptions were for five-year periods, but no more than one-third would be changed in any one adoption. This scheme prevailed as free textbooks became available for all elementary schools in the mid-1930s, the period that marked the beginning of the end of the one-room rural school as the common school in Kentucky.

In spite of the sharp competition among the book companies and the influence exerted by the book trust in educational matters at the state level, the common schools did have access to some outstanding textbooks for most of the time. It also appears that teachers were often lenient about requiring book changes in the earlier decades. Parents who were unable to pay for textbooks could request that books be supplied by use of funds from the county courts. Still, many former scholars complain that they did not have school books.

The material read by generations of common school scholars from the old McGuffey readers provided many of the popular figures of speech at the time. Some of those figures of speech have persisted well past the use of the old readers and spellers. Who does not immediately grasp the meaning of such phrases as "Crying wolf," or "Lazy

Ned," or "Meddlesome Mattie"? How long has it been since such phrases as "waste not, want not" or "try, try again" have been heard? Nearly all references to readers used by old-time scholars refer to McGuffey's series, although books by other authors, such as Goodrich, were used at times in some districts.

In the early days of education in Kentucky, many teachers were ill prepared for their jobs, materials were scarce, and schoolrooms were crowded. As teachers began to receive more instruction in educational methods, they gradually began to use the phonetic approach to reading, which for the most part held sway in common schools until the whole-word recognition was introduced. As early as 1878, in his annual report Henderson had encouraged the picture or word method of teaching reading. The timing of this approach and the use of pictures as part of the method of word recognition might suggest some association with the trend for "object teaching" (popularly spoken of as "teaching with things") that gained some currency in Louisville schools during that decade. But the phonetic approach continued to be used many years after Henderson's suggestion.

Early instruction in writing was severely handicapped by lack of facilities and materials in the pioneer schools. In the earliest days of common schools, teachers wrote the letters on crude blackboards for pupils to imitate. Rough writing desks were built along the walls of log schoolhouses for use by pupils. After improved seats with attached desks came into use, pupils worked with bottles of ink (often homemade) and quill pens. Teachers set copy on slate or paper for each individual pupil to imitate. As textbooks came into common use, various publishers offered copy books that provided model letters, words, and sentences to be copied by students on blank pages. Copy books also emphasized the "morals and manners" approach to education by the use of maxims, proverbs, and quotations in the model lessons provided. Pupils would learn to make letters and spell words, but they also gained familiarity with such gems of wisdom as "Honesty is the best policy," "Procrastination is the thief of time," and "To err is human; to forgive, divine" from the same page of exercises.

Writing had always been included in the 3 Rs as one of the absolute minimum essentials for an education. Parents on the frontier who knew the need for literacy from firsthand experience always respected the ability to "write with a good hand." Respect for this fundamental skill was transmitted to the common schools and perpetuated by the efforts of generations of masters and pupils. Schoolmasters who excelled at penmanship enjoyed excellent reputations for their accomplishments and often earned supplementary pay by teaching "writing schools."

Arithmetic for the beginners meant such things as learning to count to one hundred and recognizing and writing numbers—using the chart, the blackboard, and their slates. Pupils further along in their readers would recite from lessons in primary arithmetic, Ray's textbook being the one most commonly used. The goal of all true scholars was to master Ray's *Third Part Arithmetic,* and the problem of "Jones's will" was a memorable stumbling block. Assignments in arithmetic and spelling took a good part of the study time of pupils at their seats between recitations. Younger pupils had to learn the multiplication table.

Imaginative teachers provided their pupils with practical applications of their new knowledge. Gordon Wilson recalled such a teacher in the old Fidelity School in Calloway County. As a challenge the teacher asked Gordon to find the volume of the stovepipe. This time the answer was not in the back of the book, so he brought a tapeline from home, measured the pipe, and calculated the volume using the formula from the textbook. From this exercise the young scholar understood that mensuration applied to real objects and had practical usefulness.

This insight stimulated his interest in such matters as percentage and square root.[2]

Spelling always held an important place in the daily program of the common school. Parents, pupils, and teachers all respected a good speller. When spelling classes were called, the scholars lined up before the teacher's table. The teacher pronounced a word to the pupil at the head of the line and the scholar spelled it aloud, by syllables, pronouncing each before going on to the next one, and finally pronouncing the completed word. If the pupil spelled the word correctly he remained in place; if he missed, the next pupil got the chance to spell it and, if successful, exchanged places with the one who had missed. This process went on until the assigned lesson was completed. Pupils remembered their positions from day to day. The pupil who got the "head mark" went to the bottom the next day and started up again. Teachers usually kept a record of the head marks and gave modest prizes for the highest number in a given month—perhaps a colored pencil or some other useful but inexpensive item. The urge to excel in spelling through head marks was one of the incentives that led many students to strive for perfect attendance at school. A day of absence meant beginning at the foot of the line again.

Old-timers never failed to mention the old "Blue-Backed Speller" in their talk of school days. In the earliest years of the common schools, pupils felt they had reached a significant goal when they moved past the word *baker*, and to say that someone "never got past baker" was to make light of his academic accomplishments. Instruction in spelling during these years was rudimentary with emphasis upon syllabification and crude memory work. As teachers gained in sophistication, instruction came to include definitions of words, analysis of words (prefixes, suffixes, etc.), rules for spelling, and some elementary work in phonetics (diacritical marking), much of which would prove a mystery to the students and teachers of modern-day schools.

One of the problems faced by the common schools was to make the curriculum practical—to show the pupil that what he learned at school would be useful in life. A story by the late jurist and raconteur Judge H. H. Tye of Williamsburg illustrates his thrilling discovery of this truth. Judge Tye was known as an accomplished speller in his school. One Saturday when he was cutting sprouts in the field, Hank, the hired man, complained of the "rheumatiz." As they discussed possible remedies they recalled the name of a patent medicine that was regularly advertised in the weekly paper. When they went to the house for dinner, the young scholar started a letter to the company to order a bottle of the medicine. He turned to Hank and asked how to spell rheumatiz. Hank replied, "Why, you know how to spell it. I heard you studying your spelling book the other night and you spelled it good." At that moment, it dawned upon the future judge that what he was learning at school would be useful in life.

Written spelling lessons involved correct spelling of a word, by syllables, with all vowels marked, and giving the definition. Sometimes the teacher required that each word be used in a sentence. Written lessons were usually assigned in advance so the pupils would have time to prepare them. Spelling lessons and learning the multiplication table were almost the only assignments given children for homework in most schools of the past century.

The intermediate and advanced pupils had grammar lessons. The former used a primary text; grammar texts used by advanced students had a long development in Kentucky schools. One of the best known was by a Kentucky author, Noble Butler, and published in Louisville. Grammar texts by Thomas W. Harvey proved popular in the 1890s and the early 1900s and many scholars testified to their struggles with the twenty-two rules that had to be mastered. They studied parts of speech, declension, and conjugation, and drew elaborate diagrams on the blackboard. Although grammar was not a popular subject in the old common schools, it received a great deal of attention. To be known as a grammarian was a mark of distinction.

Despite the heavy emphasis placed on rules of grammar, techniques for analyzing speech, and structural study of language, all this had little effect on the actual speech patterns of the pupils. Immediately after an advanced grammar class had filled the blackboard with elaborate diagrams of sentences and quoted rules for their authority, it was not uncommon for the teacher to hear something like this: "Mr. Smith, can me and Tom bring in the next bucket of coal?"[3] Usually the request was understood well enough to bring an affirmative reply.

Relatively little is reported by old-timers about the other subjects that were taught in common schools. In geography classes pupils learned the capitals and boundaries of states and foreign nations and did some drawing of maps. History teaching tended to emphasize the memorization of facts and dates connected with famous events, wars, and the nation's presidents. Physiology meant learning the number and names of the bones and muscles of the body and other factual information. Some efforts were made to instruct pupils about the dangers in the use of alcohol and tobacco. Later textbooks tended to stress good health habits and practices.

In the early decades teachers often endeavored to provide some instruction for advanced scholars in other subjects. Forrest Calico, the late historian from Garrard County, recalled the extra time spent by his teachers in instructing him in some subjects not prescribed for the common schools. "I had wonderful teachers, never a poor one. One teacher brought helps into the school, mainly books of her own. Teachers would usually teach any book you would bring. I studied algebra and English history by taking these books to school."

Here and there in little white schoolhouses pupils benefited from teachers who had imagination and wide interest. A lady from Spencer County recalled her creative and talented teacher who was greatly admired and respected. This schoolmarm set a familiar poem from one of their readers to music which the pupils learned to sing with great enjoyment. Many lovers of the old-time readers will recall the words with which the poem and the song opened:

> *Twenty froggies went to school*
> *Down beside the rushy pool,*
> *Twenty coats all white and clean,*
> *Twenty desks all fresh and green.*

Teachers of early common schools who had never darkened the door of a college or normal school, or even a high school, often used plain old ingenuity to compensate for the lack of needed equipment. A poplar plank could be used as a substitute for a slate or a tablet; once used, it could quickly be shaved off with a pen knife and used again to write and "figger" on. Pens were trimmed from goose quills that could be found in nearly every barnyard. Ink could be made from elderberries, although it tended to develop an unpleasant odor if kept too long. Lacking a timepiece, a Letcher County pedagogue cut notches in the doorstep, which faced east. When the sun reached the first notch, it was time for books; the second one marked time for morning recess; and the third brought the dinner hour. Notches on a window on the west side marked time for books again, afternoon recess, and dismissal for the day.[4] Perhaps the teacher and pupils developed other dependable signals to follow on cloudy days.

Review of the old-time school program could lead to the conclusion that the emphasis was on memorization and literal adherence to rules in most subjects. This was doubtless true for most teachers and schools in the early decades during which the system was developed.

Teachers of those days had precious little in the way of preparation for teaching. Most knew only what they had been taught and the manner in which that subject matter had been handled by their instructors. It was not until two years before the common school system was modified in 1908 that the state provided facilities for teacher preparation. In view of the situation most of the teachers faced, it appears that the affection and respect accorded by their pupils were well deserved.

5

TEACHER, TEACHER, DON'T WHIP ME!

No DISCUSSION of old-time common schools is complete without considering the matter of discipline. There was a strong consensus among the people of Kentucky's agrarian society that discipline was an essential part of education. Parents and preachers and pedagogues all believed that the young should be brought up to fear the Lord—and the rod, if need be—for their own good. For most of its history, the common school had the support of parents who wanted their children to learn discipline, even if that meant chastening by the teachers. Few accounts of school days by former scholars mention any adverse reaction of their parents to punishment by teachers until those of recent decades. In fact, most people recall that their parents had promised to give them a whipping at home if they received one at school.

Accounts of experiences in common schools devote considerable space to the matter of pupil misbehavior and resultant punishment, but serious infractions of school rules and wanton misbehavior were actually exceptions rather than the rule in the vast majority of schools. People tended to recall unusual and dramatic episodes rather than the times that passed without undue incident. In most communities the traditional attempt of the "big bad boys" to run off the new teacher had, with few exceptions, gradually become a thing of the past by the end of the nineteenth century.

Common-school teachers inherited a tradition of strict discipline from the neighborhood schools that served the people before 1838. Patrons, trustees, school commissioners, and even the pupils knew the code of conduct expected in the schools. Many teachers who served in the earliest common schools, however, were ill prepared to provide competent instruction, and this tended to intensify their problem of maintaining control over an uncomfortable, crowded roomful of children, especially during the hot days of summer and early fall. All too often the only measures known to these undertrained, underpaid pedagogues were repression and corporal punishment. This tradition was gradually modified and replaced as teachers became better educated.

Teachers in old-time schools with few exceptions used rules to control the conduct of pupils, a tradition that was continued by the common schools. In 1877 the Kentucky Department of Education, under Superintendent Henderson, issued *The Kentucky School Lawyer* for the guidance of teachers; some of the suggestions dealt with discipline and pupil behavior:

Section 8—The teacher shall aim at such discipline as would be exercised by a judicious parent in his family; and in no case shall resort be had to cruel or unusual punishment as a mode of discipline.

Section 15—All communications of pupils in the schoolroom, by whispering, talking, or otherwise except by permission of the teacher is positively forbidden.

The promulgation and enforcement of rules varied widely among teachers, ranging all the way from a general statement that all pupils were expected to conduct themselves like little ladies and gentlemen to extensive, meticulous lists intended to catalog every possible misdemeanor and its penalties. Most teachers contented themselves with brief lists that dealt only with those behavior problems which their experience had taught them to expect and to be prepared to deal with.

Rules were written out in longhand, usually on sheets of tablet paper, and tacked up on the wall or by the water cooler where the pupils could note them. Most teachers read and explained the rules on the first day of school, and older pupils were instructed to explain the rules to the younger children who could not read the list for themselves. The rules most frequently recalled by former common school scholars dealt primarily with tardiness, moving about in the schoolroom, whispering, disturbing other pupils, passing notes, and being excused from the room.

Occasionally the promulgation of a rule led to its being broken. In one schoolhouse there was an opening or scuttle-hole in the ceiling to give entrance into the loft. No one had ever paid any attention to it until a new teacher forbade pupils to climb up through that scuttle-hole into the loft. Then he announced, "I am going home to lunch now and I don't want to hear of anyone climbing up through that hole." The challenge had to be met. Immediately after they had eaten their lunch, the bigger boys climbed up, and then helped up the smaller children. When the teacher returned, the last urchin was disappearing through the scuttle-hole into the loft. Punishment with a hickory stick was forthcoming, as expected, but the call to adventure had been too strong to resist.

Sometimes an ingenious pupil would come up with a novel act of misbehavior that was not covered by the current rules. When that happened in one Eastern Kentucky school, the teacher drafted a new rule to cover the situation. It happened like this: "One lad brought buttermilk to school to go with his dinner—brought it in a big quart whiskey bottle. Well, another boy slipped around and put a grasshopper in the bottle. Of course, the fellow

52

ran to the teacher and told him, but there was no rule to cover this offense. So the teacher had to make a new rule, 'Thou shalt not put grasshoppers in thy neighbor's buttermilk.' "

Human nature has changed very little over the years. One former scholar summed it up succinctly:

We did things to annoy teachers just as children do today. Often we were bored and lacked enough to do to keep us busy. We seldom did much homework as there was plenty of time to get your study done at school. Many apples were eaten behind those great big geography books, and some kids crunched on chestnuts during books time. We passed notes and there were always some romances going among the older pupils.

Once we spent all one dinner hour catching June bugs and putting them in match boxes. Back in school we took turns letting them go. We almost broke up school that warm afternoon.

A lengthy catalog of misbehavior and pranks that incurred the ire of teachers could be compiled from the recollections of common school pupils. Any such list would include such serious ones as fights (some boys carried knives, though they were forbidden by most teachers); stealing; sassing the teacher; smoking on school grounds; cruel treatment of smaller children; pulling girls' hair (if they cried); lying; cheating; leaving school without permission; swearing; indecent behavior in school, on playground, or on way to and from school; tardiness (if persistent). Obviously there were differences of opinion about what constituted serious offenses among different teachers and neighborhoods.

Lesser offenses generally included talking without permission; leaving one's seat without permission; talking too loud; laughing out loud; passing notes; spitting on the floor; shooting paper wads; teasing other children; making fun of other pupils (about poor clothes, handicaps, etc.); sneaking a "chaw" (mentioned only in earlier schools); winking at girls (or boys); tardiness (if

53

occasional); sticking pins in schoolmates; tripping pupils in the aisles; pinching other students.

Occasionally the teacher met with the trustees to reach a satisfactory solution to a disciplinary problem. An example could be cited in the case of older boys who habitually carried bullets for .22 rifles in their overalls pockets. Now and then a boy could not resist the urge to slip one into the old pot-bellied stove, which soon livened things up in a sedate schoolroom. One spur-of-the-moment prank by spirited young fellows in Trimble County was to drive an old sow and her pigs into the schoolhouse. Another was to place a chestnut burr in the teacher's chair and cover it with a piece of paper. More than one person reported that an effective way to get out of school for an hour or so was to stuff the stove pipe full of paper so the schoolroom filled with smoke when the fire was started.

There were instances when the procedures and practices of teachers themselves contributed to the behavior problems of pupils. One woman reminisced that her teacher called the roll just before recess and the dinner hour. All who had not talked without permission answered "no"; those who had talked were to respond with "yes," which meant missing five minutes of playtime. One day she answered "no" when she had actually talked. Her older sister, who had to stay in that day, threatened to tell the teacher and her mother and kept this mild blackmail over her for weeks.

There was virtually unanimous agreement on the importance of discipline. Teachers were expected to act for parents during school hours and travel to and from school. Moreover, good schools required disciplined pupils. This simple theory prevailed for most of the days of the common school, but there were significant changes in the means employed by teachers to effect discipline in their schools.

In earlier decades it was generally thought that only male teachers could maintain discipline in most schools, especially when the common schools enrolled many "big boys" (some actually old enough to vote). This view tended to persist longer in some of the mountain counties. Women teachers increased in numbers in the late nineteenth century and actually were in the majority by 1890; their numbers receded in periods of financial crisis, but recovered and kept the lead early in the first decade of the new century. Nowhere was it evident that there was any general breakdown of discipline as a result of this change.

Discipline was a perennial topic of discussion in teachers' institutes and associations during the 1880s and 1890s. Some books discussed the subject of discipline in schools, but many teachers found that their own good judgment was their best resource for dealing with such problems.

One young teacher found that her dull sense of smell proved an asset in handling the prank of a mischief-maker who slipped a hunk of asafetida on the stove. Soon the pupils began to complain of the "awful smell." Requests to leave the room were refused. When the teacher proved adamant, little heads went down on their desks and illness prevailed. When time came for dismissal, the door was opened and the room gradually became more habitable. That was the only time that an ill-smelling substance was placed on the stove while that teacher was in charge.

Another case of making the punishment fit the crime was reported from Bullitt County. A lad who took the trouble to pour soap in the schoolhouse well was required to do the clean-up job. As a result he spent hours dipping out the well to clear up the school's water supply.

Efforts to discipline pupils were not always so effective. In a Marion County school one Lafey Harmon jumped out the window to get away from an ear pulling by the teacher, who followed and chased Lafey for about a mile before he gave up and returned without him.

Although the discipline problem gradually eased in

common schools over the years, some teachers still had to show much "intestinal fortitude." An old-timer told about such a case: "One man teacher was run off by some older boys who wouldn't study. It got so he couldn't turn his back to use the blackboard—the bad boys threw everything at him—he couldn't control them. The trustees brought in another man—they 'knowed' him before he came—he was a one-armed man but laid the law down—the bad boys laid out of school and stopped coming."

Teachers used a variety of punishments for disciplinary purposes in the common schools. Former pupils recall firsthand experiences of many of these methods with varying degrees of enthusiasm and feeling.

Whipping stands first in almost any respect, with switches, paddles, pointers, rulers, yardsticks, straps, belts, and light canes used against knuckles, open hands, around shoulder blades, lower back, across buttocks, and around the calves. Whipping was administered with the child either bending over or standing up straight; in a few cases it was given to the child bending across a chair or desk or even across the knees of an irate pedagogue. Some teachers kept a switch (or a bundle) handy, ready for instant application, others delayed the whipping to extend its anticipatory effect, and still others sent the victim to procure an appropriate instrument for the punishment.

Standing-in-the-corner was a frequent penalty, used for many kinds of offenses, mostly minor, and it could be varied by requiring the culprit to stand on only one foot or to lean his weight against the wall on one hand. A variation of this method was to require a pupil to stand and keep his nose in a ring drawn on the blackboard.

Dunce stools and dunce caps were traditional means of giving mild punishment to pupils in schools of colonial and pioneer days but appear to have been used only very early and rarely in Kentucky common schools. Only a few former scholars mention either device.

The taking away of playtime (keeping pupils in during

recess or dinner hour) was used occasionally by some teachers, but unless teachers stayed in too it probably did little good, and everyone needed that midmorning break.

Keeping children after school was an effective measure, since most pupils had to explain a late arrival home to their parents. The time assigned to be spent after school varied according to the severity of the offense. One informant remembered that he once acquired a whole week of this punishment and grew very tired of it. Another told about a teacher whose memory was faulty. The youngster was instructed to stay in after school, which he did. Soon the teacher left the schoolroom and promptly forgot about him. She went home, leaving the youth all by himself. Finally, as dark approached, he got up and hurried home. Strangely, he never received any explanation, but he and his folks thought the teacher rather absentminded.

A common form of punishment was to require pupils to memorize a poem or a column from the big dictionary. Several scholars still recall this experience after many years, and not one of them felt that it had increased his appreciation of good literature or his vocabulary.

Many teachers sought to inhibit misbehavior by requiring the culprit to write "I will not [fill in the crime]" 500 times on the blackboard or in a tablet. Sometimes the teacher required the pupils to copy several pages from the dictionary or to copy some long word, such as accountability, several hundred times.

Teachers discovered several effective ways to deal with the forbidden practice of writing and passing notes to one's sweetheart. In some schools the writer had to stand and read the missive aloud to the entire school; elsewhere the teacher read it, and in some schools the message was written on the blackboard.

One excruciatingly painful form of punishment for little boys, especially those who were shy, was to remove them from their own seats down front and plant them in a seat between two "grown girls." It worked in many cases, but it certainly did nothing to enhance the teacher's image among the little boys.

Some forms of punishment recalled by former pupils were more unusual. One teacher required miscreants to kneel down on a broom handle which doubtless soon made one resolve to do better or at least not to get caught. Another teacher made a schoolgirl hold soda, salt, and pepper in her mouth for telling a fib about cheating. Still another teacher moved mischievous pupils into seats with children from a family that was known to be "lousy," a plan that was quite effective.

Scholars voiced the impression that male teachers often whipped pupils for certain forms of misbehavior that female teachers punished by keeping in after school. A number felt that male and female teachers alike tended to get angry when pupils talked back to them. Most scholars thought that punishment for failure to complete one's lessons often did more harm than good. It was also noted that the form of punishment was not so important as the attitude of the teacher toward the pupil who was being disciplined. Many pupils were concerned about what their teachers—those they liked and respected—thought of them and believed about them. Most old-timers would have agreed with the statement of one of their number about the approach to discipline preferred by the best teachers: "My best teacher talked to pupils about their conduct and encouraged them to do right."

Teachers who appeared to play favorites in their treatment of pupils were certain to be resented by the other pupils. Most teachers tried to be consistent, but it was not always easy. Those teachers who boarded with a family in the neighborhood had to take care to avoid any semblance of partiality to pupils from that home. Often those pupils felt that the teacher required more of them than of others. Teachers were likewise vulnerable to any charges of favoritism toward the children of the trustees. No quicker way to criticism and a one-year career in that school could be found.

Former common-school pupils vividly recalled episodes in which they were involved. Many persons still carried strong feelings about unfair treatment at the hands of former teachers. An elderly farmer in Garrard County still resented unfair punishment by a teacher who whipped him for a fight with another pupil but did not discipline his opponent. Since the teacher was then courting the other boy's older sister, the pupils believed this explained the inconsistent treatment. This same teacher used an unusual method of punishing the girls. Sticks were placed in their mouths and tied by strings that reached around back of the head. One boy who failed to spell loud enough to suit this schoolmaster was made to stand outside in the schoolyard and yell the letters loud enough to be heard by the teacher inside. Two words, *survive* and *adopt,* were spelled twenty-five times each in this manner and never forgotten by this youngster.

An elderly former pupil of a common school for black children located outside of Paris vividly recalled an episode that contributed to his decision to leave school at an early age. By his own account it appears that he presented some problems for his teachers. "I was so devilish that teachers sent letters to my home about my conduct. So my father made a paddle for the teacher to use on me, put five holes in it. I got one whipping with it. The lady teacher put me over an old chair—one with the back broken off—and hit one lick. That was enough. I lunged at her and knocked her down. That made her so mad she really hit me hard and that really hurt. So I just rammed my head between her legs and bit her on one leg."

This and some other episodes about that time caused the boy to leave school and get a job in a grocery store. The happy ending is that he studied at nights and educated himself to the eighth-grade level.

In the late decades of the common school, the discipline problem declined significantly. Accounts of behavior of pupils during the 1920s and 1930s sound quite different from those of the 1890s. A number of factors could have contributed to this trend. Teachers were better educated for their tasks. The school day was less boring and tedious, with new activities and materials that interested children. An important change was that the late teenagers and young adults were no longer in elementary schools. Certainly some schools and some teachers still had to cope with behavior problems, but in general the days of rip-roaring stunts and harsh punitive measures were past. One pupil from a rural one-room school during the 1930s recalled the situation briefly: "We had hardly any misbehavior at all. We did not have any real problems. We knew what was expected of us and did not give the teacher any real trouble; we knew that we would be paddled if we did."

One local historian found an old rhyme that commented upon the harsh discipline in old-time schools:

> Method and discipline would sometimes mix,
> And generally to the tune of hickory sticks;
> Teachers could not be said to be really mean,
> They simply loved to run a "thrashing machine."[1]

6

PLAYTIME, GAMETIME

THE PLAY EXPERIENCES of pupils represented the most pleasurable aspect of their common school careers for most old-time scholars. No matter how dreary the environment, how tiresome the long hours of books, how strict the teacher, how few the books and other instructional materials, or how rough the daily walk to school, the time spent outside at play was nearly always recalled with pleasure and enthusiasm. Games that have disappeared over the years come to life in descriptions of how to play town round, or ante-over, or shinny, or ring men, or any one of a dozen others.[1] Tales of prowess in sports, of victories over rivals, and of long-absent teammates bring back vivid scenes from the past.

The pupils of the old-time common school played happily and vigorously without the space and equipment considered necessary for playgrounds and play activities of modern schools. No matter how tired and dispirited pupils may have felt during books, the welcome sound of the bell that signaled recess brought instant rejuvenation as boys and girls alike rushed outside for fun and recreation. This was one phase of their school life that was generally under their control.

Games recalled from the schools of a century ago clearly show how the pupils used whatever they could find for their amusement in the school environment. Boys from schools along the rivers and creeks frequently skated when the streams froze over. A few former pupils remembered times when even the Ohio froze over solid and they had great fun skating. Smaller children often played along the creek or river banks and built sand structures. This led to parental concern about safety near deep spots and the danger of water moccasins, or cotton-mouths, as they were called in some parts of the state.

High banks along the sides of the road were used for many activities—digging, sliding, and mock battles. Sometimes the banks were burrowed or tunneled into by young engineers. Many schoolhouses stood next to woods, which offered a variety of recreational facilities. A young hickory sapling could be climbed and the top bent over by a venturesome lad until other pupils could reach it and turn it into an acceptable "ridey horse." Sometimes a board could be balanced across a stump or fallen tree trunk to make a usable seesaw for younger children. Branches, dead sticks, and leaves could be fashioned into rude but satisfactory playhouses for the smaller girls. Leaves from hickory saplings could be pinned together by their own stems to make hats or clothes for stick dolls.

The luxuriant growth of wild grapevines in the forests provided much pleasure to pupils of early schools. Jump ropes would most likely be made from these grapevines. More exciting was to fashion a swing from a strong vine by cutting it loose near the ground and hanging onto it to swing like a pendulum. This was a favorite pastime for country boys around their swimming holes. One could swing back and forth, finally letting go to land with a splash in the middle of the creek or river. A scholar of the old Low Gap School in Magoffin County still marvels that no one drowned from their swings out over the river at the end of a long grapevine, nearly ninety years ago.

Ball games were popular where there was enough open and level space available. The girls played townball or town round, as some called it, particularly when there were few boys attending the school. When the teacher took an active part on the playground, this tended to increase the girls' participation. Some girls developed a sharp eye for batting the soft yarn ball with the flat bat commonly used, and they were quickly picked when the two captains chose up sides.

"Choosing up" was a ritual, and getting the first choice required good judgment, coordination, and manual dexterity. One captain tossed the bat to the other, who caught it in mid-air and held it out before him, not moving his handhold. The two captains alternated handholds until the one who held the top grip got the first choice for his side. Sometimes the last grip was so precarious, merely a fingerhold, that possession was challenged, whereupon the claimant had to toss the bat into the air over his head. If successful, he had the first choice.

Being chosen first or near the top gave prestige, while being chosen last or not at all brought humiliation. Many children too young to have achieved the coordination needed for batting, catching, and throwing would gladly have traded prized possessions, the best-loved dinner, or their scholastic talents to be able to hit a home run or to throw the side out. One scholar told how she would catch the ball in her apron. She liked to play and devised this means of helping her team, but it caused a lot of arguments—which never settled permanently the question of its legality.

Schools that lacked space to play townball could always use the schoolhouse itself for a rousing game of ante-over. Hide-and-seek could be managed in most physical environments, as could marble games, hat ball, dare-base, leap-frog, froggy-in-the-meadow, whipcracker, squat tag, three-deep, and many others. The little girls might choose singing games such as London bridge, farmer-in-the-dell, or mulberry bush, or they might jump rope to any one of numerous jingles that most scholars still recall after many years. Teenage boys and girls often played games such as drop-the-handkerchief or one of its variations, which afforded pleasant experiences with the opposite sex without risk of being teased. And there were always fields, streams, and woods, with all kinds of hazards for uphill and downdale chases of fox-and-hound. These distance-running games often took the youth over courses that could have been counted in miles, at times taking them so far from the school that they were late in getting back.

After consolidation began and the number of high schools proliferated, the rural schools adopted games that have been universally popular throughout the Commonwealth. Baseball was played in some schools, but was limited generally by the lack of equipment and enough big boys. Volleyball found its way into some schools and proved popular with both boys and girls, especially after county school fairs came into vogue. As these fairs became common, many pupils eagerly prepared to enter into the track and field events that were scheduled for rural school pupils. But the favorite new sport turned out to be basketball. By the 1920s and 1930s passersby could see basketball goals mounted on trees, the nearby coalhouse, and a variety of posts at rural schoolhouses across the state. Funds raised by the annual box or pie suppers were often used to purchase basketballs for would-be stars on the rough outdoor courts.

A few games popular with older teenage pupils were not permitted by some teachers, usually because of parental objections. These were the games played at "play-parties" in neighborhoods that permitted old-time square dances. Parents often objected to these so-called kissing games. In some schools older boys and girls would leave the school grounds to play Buffalo gal, go-in-and-out-the-window, King William, Roxie-Ann, or the Virginia reel (the last not actually a kissing game, but likewise tainted by its common use at play-parties).

Many different games were played in common schools,

most of which appeared to be known throughout the state. Six that were traditional favorites were played in some counties as long as one-room schools lasted.

Ante-over was a simple game that would accommodate any number of players, big and little. The equipment consisted of a rag ball, and the play space was the area immediately around the schoolhouse. There was an advantage if the schoolhouse rested upon cornerstones high enough to enable the players to see under the building and get advance warning that their opponents were coming. Sides were chosen up by two captains, or a few players would volunteer to oppose the rest of the school. Each team then took one side of the building; the side with the ball yelled "Ante," the others replied "Over," and then the ball was thrown. If it was caught by the receiving side, those players would rush around the schoolhouse and throw the ball at opponents. Those hit by the rag ball had to join the opposite team. If the ball was not caught, the same procedure was followed from the opposite side of the schoolhouse. The game required little, but involved all who chose to play and gave the children exercise, the thrill of escape, and fun to boot; these advantages were obviously the clues to its popularity.

Dare-base was usually played by older pupils who would divide into two groups. Each group stood behind a line facing the other across an open space. A member of one team would approach the line in front of the opponent as closely as possible, but the moment he touched that line the opponent tried to touch him, in which case he was captured and returned with the captors. Touching the line, however, constituted a dare for the defending team, and when they essayed forth to catch the darer they could be caught by his teammates, who could come out into the open space to aid him.

A perennial favorite was drop-the-handkerchief. It could include pupils of all ages, it offered some contact with one's "sweetie" without incurring the ire of patrons

65

and teachers who opposed "kissing games," it accommodated any number of players, and it gave rise to few arguments among the players. Some variations were reported; one from Pike County was played with a verse sung as the player circled the ring:

> *I lost my glove yesterday,*
> *And found it today;*
> *Found it full of water*
> *And threw it away.*

A glove or some other object was stealthily dropped behind someone in the ring of players during the singing. The chosen person was then to pick up the glove, chase and tag the one who dropped it. If he was successful in making the tag, the first person was still "it." If he was unsuccessful, he became "it."

Froggy-in-the-meadow was popular with the younger children. Everyone forms a circle and walks around with closed eyes; "Froggy" is in the center and all chant two or three times: "Froggy's in the meadow and can't get out; Take a little stick and poke him about. Where's Froggy?" While the circle moves and chants, "Froggy" leaves the middle and hides. With the last verse, all open their eyes and look for "Froggy." When he is found, the discoverer gets to be the next "Froggy."

Among the singing games, some were known as kissing games. One of the most popular, especially among the teenagers was go-in-and-out-the-window. Players join hands and form a circle, except for the couple chosen to be "it." The children in the circle raise their hands so these two can go in and out of the circle while the first verse is sung by all.

> *Go in and out the window*
> *Go in and out the window*
> *Go in and out the window*
> *Since we have gained this day.*

66

(The boy who has been going "in and out the window" stands and faces his partner while the second verse is sung.)

> *Stand forth and face your lover*
> *Stand forth and face your lover*
> *Stand forth and face your lover*
> *Since we have gained this day.*

(The boy kneels before his partner as the third verse is sung.)

> *I'll kneel because I love you*
> *I'll kneel because I love you*
> *I'll kneel because I love you*
> *Since we have gained this day.*

(The boy shows how to measure his love by stretching his arms while still kneeling while the fourth verse is sung.)

> *I'll measure my love to show you*
> *I'll measure my love to show you*
> *I'll measure my love to show you*
> *Since we have gained this day.*

(The boy then runs and tries to catch his partner while the last verse is sung.)

> *I'll break my neck to kiss you*
> *I'll break my neck to kiss you*
> *I'll break my neck to kiss you*
> *Since we have gained this day.*

(As last verse ends, action is suited to the word.)

No game played by common school pupils was more universally loved than needle's eye with its catchy tune. Two pupils (captains) face each other and raise their joined hands as in London bridge; the others join hands in a circle and march around, going between the two captains, while the first verse is sung:

> *Needle's eye, that doth supply*
> *The thread that runs so true,*

67

> *Many a beau have I let go*
> *Because I wanted you.*

The two captains, holding hands high, form the needle's eye; the children marching through become the thread. With the last word, "you," the captains drop hands, catching one of the children. This one they take off to one side and ask whether he or she would rather be, for example, a red bird or a blue bird. The pupil then catches that captain around the waist. The game continues in the same way as the children sing the second verse:

> *Many a dark and stormy night*
> *As I walked home with you*
> *I'd stub my toe and down I'd go*
> *Because I wanted you.*

The game proceeds, with first and second verses sung alternately, until all are caught, after which the two lines hold a tug-of-war.

Many of the games and physical activities once enjoyed by children have lost favor with school children of recent years. One rarely sees or hears of the popular games played with various kinds of marbles in old-time common schools, games such as ringmen, rolly-hole, and keeps. Old-timers recall the days when every boy had different kinds of marbles in his overalls pockets—large white ringmen, taws, steel balls, and agates—and keeps by the dozen. Possession of a good taw was a matter of prestige, and to be a good shot was even better. Some boys played so often and so hard that they wore grooves in the thumb-nail of their shooting hand.

Among other traditional games that have disappeared along with the little white schoolhouse are mumblety-peg, roll-the-hoop, pitching washers, whip-cracker, and several "base" games.

Certain games reported by former scholars appear to have an interesting historical background. A former teacher in Pike County schools described a singing game played by her mother and still current in the old Barrenshea School on Tug Fork as late as the mid-1930s. This school, long since consolidated, had thirty pupils in 1936, all of whom answered to one of three family names: Chapman, Lane, or Norman. Lady Fair was a circle game in which first one boy, then another, stood before the girl of his choice and brought her into the center of the circle as the players sang:

> *In this ring a lady fair,*
> *Deep blue eyes and curly brown hair,*
> *Rosy cheeks and dimpled chin,*
> *Choose your partner and she'll come in.*
>
> *Now you're married, you're married for life,*
> *Law, law, law, what a pretty little wife!*
> *Pretty little wife, and husband, too,*
> *Kiss her once and that will do.*

King William, a singing game, must have an intriguing history.[2] It was played by children holding hands and walking in a circle, with one child in the center:

> *King William was King George's son,*
> *So the royal race is run,*
> *On his breast he wore a star,*
> *In his mouth a big cigar;*
> *Go choose to the East, go choose to the West,*
> *Choose the one you love the best;*
> *If she's not here to take her part,*
> *Choose another with all your heart.*

(Player in the center suited actions to the words as sung.)

Kentucky is a long way from the place and time of the King William IV to whom this ditty refers. How this game was brought to certain common schools is an interesting subject for speculation and research.

Jumping rope has always been a favorite form of play for little schoolgirls, whether they used grapevines or any of a variety of kinds of rope, including fancy commercial types. Through the long history of the amusement an amazing tradition of jump-rope jingles has developed. Observers of the relaxed rhythmic play have recognized its place in the playtime of the pupils. Rhyme, rhythm, rituals, and recreation are all involved. Many have continued on into modern schools and others will doubtless be composed each year. Some of the old favorites are:

Down in the meadow where the green grass grows,
There sat (Susie) *pretty as a rose.*
She sang and she sang and she sang so sweet.
Along came (Johnny) *and kissed her on the cheek.*
How many kisses did she get that week?

(Throw "hot" to see how many kisses she got.)

Johnny over the ocean,
Johnny over the sea.
Johnny broke a milk bottle,
And blamed it on me.
How many spankings did Johnny get?

Johnny over the ocean,
Johnny over the sea.
Johnny had a secret
He told on me.
How many secrets did Johnny tell?

Not last night, but the night before,
Twenty-four robbers came knocking at my door.
I ran out as they ran in,
And this is what they said to me:
  Spanish Lady turn around,
  Spanish Lady touch the ground,
  Spanish Lady hop up and down,
  Spanish Lady get out of town.

Peel an orange round and round,
Peel a banana upside down.

70

If I jump to twenty-four,
I will get my turn once more.

(Throw "hot" and count to twenty-four or until the jumper misses.)

Cinderella dressed in yellow
Went upstairs to see her fellow.
She made a mistake and kissed a snake.
How many doctors did it take?

I'm a little Dutch girl dressed in blue.
These are the things I like to do:
    Salute to the Captain,
    Curtsy to the Queen,
    Turn myself like a washing-machine.

(The pupil jumping suits action to the words chanted.)

Teddy Bear Teddy Bear turn around
Teddy Bear Teddy Bear touch the ground
Teddy Bear Teddy Bear show your shoes
Teddy Bear Teddy Bear read the news
Teddy Bear Teddy Bear go be excused.

(The pupil jumping acts out each part as it is sung. On the line "go be excused" the jumper runs out and another runs in, starting the jingle over again.)

Sometimes the children jumped to the rule of "don't leave the cookie jar empty"—in which as soon as one child finished a jingle and jumped out, another jumped in immediately, so as not to "leave the cookie jar empty." Sometimes no jingle at all was used and children simply counted how many times they could jump without missing. Other games included stacking books—in which the rope was not turned, but simply raised higher and higher until the jumper could no longer jump over it.

Bad weather posed problems for everyone at playtime, especially during the dinner hour. It had to be a heavy rain to force the hardiest spirits indoors. Snow kept few inside; it merely provided opportunity for some different

71

activities which most pupils enjoyed even at the risk of wet shoes and parental displeasure. Most teachers left pupils to make their own choices except when parents had given instructions that their children were not to play outside in bad weather. These pupils usually resented the restriction, for they dreaded the taunts of schoolmates. Older girls, more concerned about their hair and clothes, were less likely to mind staying indoors.

Indoor activities during the dinner hour were a problem for most teachers. Some left the situation unstructured, taking action only to keep things under control. Many teachers tried to minimize the problems that arose from a crowded room and restless pupils by shortening the time for recess periods and dinner and having an early dismissal. The teachers tried to promote games and activities that would keep all but one of the pupils in their seats at any one time. A few teachers introduced recreational activities, such as storytelling, round songs, simple calisthenics, and indoor games. Such games as charades, cross-questions-and-crooked-answers, thimble, and guessing games were tried by more enterprising teachers. Other games were devised to use the blackboard for simple exercises that pupils enjoyed doing in competition. Some of these have been observed in the few one-room schools that continue to operate in the 1970s.

Former pupils of one-room rural schools almost universally recall playtime as the most satisfying aspect of their common school experience. Despite the lack of adequate playing spaces, playground equipment, blacktop surfaces, and trained supervisors, the boys and girls from the farms and hamlets found means of amusing themselves with games and equipment largely of their own devising. The great number (over a hundred) of games and play activities recalled by former pupils indicates that children found fun and relief from the school routine at least three times a day.

"Book time" in a mountain
school, about 1930
*Courtesy of
Alice Lloyd College, Photo-
graphic Archives*

Top: John Banks and his class, Letcher County, 1930 *Courtesy of Mrs. Louama Gibson Banks Bottom:* The walk home from a Breathitt County school, 1940 *Courtesy of Farm Security Administration*

A dilapidated school
in Crittenden County, 1956
*Reprinted with permission
from* THE COURIER-JOURNAL
AND THE LOUISVILLE TIMES

Owsley County
Teachers' Institute, 1894
James W. Steele Papers.
Courtesy of C. Leland Smith

Christmas at a school
in Spencer County, 1930s
Courtesy of
Mrs. Sue Dent Taber

A geography lesson at Murphy School in Wolfe County, 1945. The recitation benches were made in the early 1900s. *Reprinted with permission from* THE COURIER-JOURNAL AND THE LOUISVILLE TIMES

10. The fur of the beaver is highly prized. The men who hunt these animals are called trappers.

11. A gentleman once saw five young beavers playing. They would leap on the trunk of a tree that lay near a beaver dam, and would push one another off into the water.

12. He crept forward very cautiously, and was about to fire on the little creatures; but their amusing tricks reminded him so much of some little children he knew at home, that he thought it would be inhuman to kill them. So he left them without even disturbing their play.

a, 3.

Page from McGuffey's *Third Eclectic Reader* (New York: American Book Company, 1920)

Top: Recess at a rural school of the 1970s   *Bottom:* Carrying water to the schoolhouse, 1965   *Reprinted with permission from* THE COURIER-JOURNAL AND THE LOUISVILLE TIMES

7

OUTSIDE OF BOOKS

THE OLD KENTUCKY common school contributed to the educational development of its pupils both during and outside the time of books. The role of the common school in providing formal schooling is clear. But its function—informal and unplanned though it was—in providing the place and the times for many other kinds of education was also significant. How many children of tender age got their disillusionment of the Santa Claus myth from more sophisticated youngsters of the same age at the neighborhood school? Or the one about the doctor bringing babies? How many little boys from homes that observed strict standards of language and manners learned cuss words and "naughty" expressions in the same context? Although there are relatively few written references to this informal function of the common school, it contributed mightily to the education of its pupils. Superstitions, half-truths, old wives' tales that passed for wisdom, and maxims—all these and much more became part of the total learning experience.

Matters of health were often part of this extracurricular education. Many pupils wore amulets made of asafetida around the neck to ward off colds (actually the practice warded off togetherness). At times the teacher would draw attention to the importance of cleanliness by sending some pupils to the nearest stream or pond to bathe. This was usually followed by a request sent to the parents to clean up their children. It was effective in a few instances.

Another part of the education of a youngster in the rural Kentucky of past decades was self-defense. Nearly every school knew from experience about bullies who made life miserable for many a little boy who had no bigger brother or cousin to defend him. The need for self-defense was very real.

Nevyle Shackelford tells of an experience he had with a school bully. An older boy who had acted as Nevyle's protector quit school, and without this defender Nevyle was beaten up by the bully. When Nevyle's father saw the tearful face and damaged condition, he told the boy what to do: "Don't start anything, just go on like nothing has happened, but if he gets you down again, pick up anything you can find—anything at hand—and just kill him."

The very next morning Nevyle got to school early, before the teacher arrived. The bully came up and jumped him, pushing him down, but fortunately a piece of timber was within reach. Nevyle grabbed it and struck his tormenter hard at the ankles. The bully bent over to check the damage, whereupon Nevyle hit him on the back of the neck and laid him out cold. At that point the teacher arrived and asked what happened. Nevyle said, "I guess I killed him." The teacher checked the fallen bully, who recovered in due course, but Nevyle was not bothered after that one challenge.

Sometimes when things were dull and the bigger boys wanted to see some action, they would make a couple of little boys fight each other. The two may have had no reason to do battle, but that made no difference. The gang would crowd around, making a ring. They would start to push the two luckless lads into each other until they got bumped hard and bloodied; then one or both would lash out and a fight was on. Worst of all, the victims often got a whipping from the teacher after having been in gladiatorial combat. Many fights were entered into willingly. As one man recalled: "We had the customary fights some of which were very good. There was one fight in which I took care of a couple of boys and I felt that I should have received some kind of medal for it but the teacher disagreed."

Sex education was also furthered in some ways, though plenty of misinformation on the topic was perpetuated as well. Many pupils came to school with some elementary knowledge about sex gained from observing farm animals and overhearing adult conversations. Other pupils were much less knowledgable in the subject. The walls of the toilet provided education for some youngsters. One story of such a learning experience comes from a county on the Tennessee border. About the third year in school a little farm girl was first exposed to some four-letter words by seeing them on the toilet walls. Mystified, she went home and asked her parents what they meant. Their reaction was one of horror. It was not until some years later that she learned the meaning of the words from schoolmates, who may not have provided the most accurate knowledge. It would be impossible to compute the emotional stress and mental anguish that were caused by the horribly garbled accounts of sexual behavior and the awful predictions of what would happen to children who engaged in certain practices.[1]

Many references to "courting" in the old-time common school days prove that this was an important aspect of learning. Many school friendships ripened into love and marriage. One account of an early crush reported what must have been the learning of an antisocial skill by the lad in question, who "would steal chickens, sell them and bring me chewing gum." One of the most unusual experiences reported was that of a teenage girl who had attended school very little and was not able to write her own love letters. She would get younger girls to write them for her. She would tell them what to write, but they put down whatever they wished.

Older courting couples sometimes slipped away at the noon hour for more privacy. When a rambling crew playing fox-and-hounds blundered upon such a couple, lying in a secluded spot, a few would abandon the game in favor of something that promised more entertainment.

Some of the most interesting informal learnings were the innumerable jingles, rhymes, and singsong verses that were developed in various situations. Love-sick youth wrote them on flyleaves of textbooks, penned them on myriad notes and missives, and inscribed them in the "memory books" that became popular before common schools declined. Who could resist an impassioned declaration of deathless love?

> *You I love, and will forever.*
> *Times will change but I will never.*
> *Time will come when we must part*
> *But time can never change my heart.*

Another category of pupil lore was the jingle that could be recited rapidly in a sort of singsong voice serving a need for expression when more direct and explicit terms might have brought down the teacher's wrath. An example is:

> *Teacher! Teacher! Don't whip me;*
> *Whip that boy behind the tree.*
> *He stole sugar; I stole honey;*
> *Teacher! Teacher! Ain't that funny?*

Other versions insert "money" for "sugar," but the result was the same.

The common schools also facilitated the overall education of the people by providing a place for meetings and activities. Schoolhouses often served as polling places and also accommodated meetings of farmers' organizations; protest meetings in the 1890s against the tollgates of turnpike companies and "good roads" meetings in the early twentieth century; meetings for farmers with the county agent; 4-H Club activities (after 1914); political meetings; night classes for illiterates; traveling shows; religious meetings (with permission of the trustees); annual box or pie suppers; Friday afternoon exercises; meetings of literary and debating societies; Christmas and Last Day programs. People were encouraged to use the school as their social and cultural center.

When schools opened in the summer, most families were too busy with their farm work to attend community events. After the early weeks of the term, some of the venturesome teachers would begin to hold Friday afternoon exercises to which parents and visitors were invited. The youngest children learned and recited short pieces, intermediate pupils quoted Bible verses or gave recitations from McGuffey's *Third Reader,* and the advanced scholars staged a brief debate on a weighty subject, engaged in a dialogue, or declaimed some popular selection—"Spartacus' Address to the Gladiators," "Marco Bozzaris," or "Curfew Shall Not Ring Tonight." Such exercises were usually concluded with a full-scale spelling bee or ciphering match in which the whole school, and sometimes even the visitors, participated.

By the time crops were in and the load of farm work had eased somewhat, the teacher might ask the Friday visitors to help organize a literary society or a debating club. Local leaders were chosen and programs were arranged on a biweekly or monthly basis. A typical program included a devotional, announcements, dialogues, readings, recitations, and talks by parents, perhaps an exhibition of outstanding work by scholars, and a debate or spelling bee. Debates were held on a variety of questions, all the way from imponderables to current political topics. The debaters were known to lose their tempers in the course of debates upon such hot political issues as

77

Free Silver and the Populist movement of the 1890s. The literary societies clearly served a social purpose in rural neighborhoods.

The most popular event of the school year was the annual box or pie supper. This raised money for school equipment and provided a social event for the neighborhood. There was much fun when youthful admirers sought to purchase the boxes brought by the young ladies they fancied. Other youths would bid until they ran the price of the desired box as high as possible. Sometimes their strategy backfired, when the admirer dropped out and let the competing bidder have the box.

Young courting couples devised various ways to help the youthful admirer recognize the box or pie he coveted. At some auctions as each girl's pie was sold, she stood behind a sheet stretched as a curtain for the stage with a lamp placed behind her. The silhouette helped her admirer to know when the box he wanted was up for sale.

Early in the 1900s another popular event of the school year was the annual school fair usually held at the county seat. Many schools prepared to take part by decorating a farm wagon as a float for the parade and arranging for pupils to take part in the numerous athletic and scholastic contests. Those who devised the prettiest float received a cash prize and the even more coveted recognition that went along with it, as did the winners of the various events.

In the fall when the nuts were ripe on the chestnut, hickory, and walnut trees, many teachers took their schools on nutting expeditions. Pupils often begged for a field trip to visit an old-fashioned sorghum mill or a sawmill that might be in operation near the schoolhouse and occasionally such requests were granted.

In some districts it was customary for the teacher to take all the pupils to one daytime service during the annual revival meeting held by a neighboring Protestant church in the late summer or early fall. Legal and constitutional questions about such visitations probably never occurred to the teachers, parents, or local trustees.

Games in old-time schools were generally played on a pick-up basis, but there were also some instances of school contests at townball. Occasionally the older boys who excelled at the game would persuade their teacher, with the appropriate permission from parents and trustees, to arrange for the school to visit another school in an adjoining district to play ball and engage in a spelling match. Such a trip usually took the better part of the day. Most often the traveling school set out on foot at morning recess time in order to arrive about noon. Lunch was eaten either on the way or at the visited school. The ball game followed during most of the dinner hour.

Then all crowded into the schoolhouse for a competitive spelling match that might continue for up to two hours. Occasionally, the time was divided between spelling and ciphering matches. Both teachers gave out words and acted as judges. Usually the visitors started back to their own school or home at afternoon recess.

On pretty days the urge to get outside and away from the set routine of the school was so great that almost any break in the routine took on the attractiveness of an outing. A combined outing and project to earn money for library books was reported from one of the counties of the cotton belt in the Jackson Purchase. The teacher and pupils picked cotton for a few hours in a neighboring field and contributed their pay to the school fund for library books. Some time later this same enterprising teacher led several pupils on a possum hunt with surprising success. Twelve marsupials were bagged and sold, with the proceeds again donated to the library fund.

Christmas was the highlight of the year in many neighborhoods and in early days marked the end of the term. A cedar tree that would nearly reach the ceiling was favored in most parts of the state. It would be hung with home-made decorations, which would include strings of popcorn and chains of colored paper. Little pieces of tinsel and foil were saved for stars, and sycamore balls were dipped in a flour-and-water mixture to give them a snowy look. Gifts placed on the trees were also homemade—crocheted items, handkerchiefs, pin cushions, and knitted mittens, socks and stockings, and even scarves. After the program of recitations, readings, and carols, the gifts were distributed. Usually the teacher provided treats for everyone. Stick candy (peppermint, lemon, and horehound), fancy candy such as gumdrops, black-and-whites, chocolate drops, and sticks of wax or chewing gum were most common. Sometimes oranges were given to the pupils. When apples were plentiful, they were distributed to all the people. At some schools Santa Claus would distribute the gifts from the tree and perhaps oranges or some little gifts from his pack.

There were instances in which the long-awaited Christmas program had consequences that were neither expected nor desired. A retired teacher from Woodford County recalls a year when she and her pupils worked long and hard on their Christmas program, which was very successful. Among the packed audience in the hot, closed schoolroom, however, were children from one family who were breaking out with measles. Attendance for the remaining month of school fell drastically as every family fought off the ravages of the malady spread so effectively by the Christmas party.

It was only after the common school term was lengthened to seven months that the last day of school fell in January. Some schools made a great occasion of the last day. One of the biggest celebrations was held in the old Camp Ground School in Hart County. There were no lessons that day, just entertainment. Parents, visitors, and friends filled the schoolhouse to overflowing. People brought fiddles, guitars, accordions, hand harps, French harps, and bass fiddles, and made music galore. Songs were sung, stories were told, poems were recited; a spelling bee and arithmetic matches took place; and the teacher treated everyone to candy and fruits.

These are just a few of the many kinds of informal learning experiences offered in each and every common school in Kentucky. Many a former pupil has a hoard of special memories of what was learned outside of books.

8

TALES OUT OF SCHOOL

THE OLD KENTUCKY common school was above all an institution of the people, and as such, it reflected their way of life. It continued to do so until that way of life had been largely altered and supplanted by new ways that spelled the end of the little white schoolhouse. But to the virtual end the one-room school was an institution marked by interpersonal relationships, where successes and failures, joys and sorrows, were all shared. From this source originated an incalculable number and variety of human interest stories that depict the lives of the people as they pursued their educational goals.

One of the characteristics of the old-time common school was the monotony; hours were long and there was little activity. Pupils were overfamiliar with the same old books and the boredom of memory work. In the course of a long, tiring day, almost any incident, however trivial, would serve to break the tedium and would long be remembered.

Many stories relate experiences of being teased and annoyed by other pupils, the blame usually being placed on mischievous boys. For little girls there were many problems, some of which led to amusing outcomes. "One day while working on my arithmetic the boy behind me kept punching me with a pencil. Finally I shoved back hard to get back at him and struck my crazy bone. It hurt so bad that I screamed out as loud as I could. The teacher rushed back and asked, 'Martha, what in the world is the matter?' I answered, 'I struck my bellow.'" Name-calling, frightening the girls with snakes and bugs, and other kinds of teasing were common in the schoolyard as well as on the walks to and from school.

There was no hard and fast line between teasing and what was often called devilment. One bit of what must be called devilment took place in a little white schoolhouse near Pattieville in Ohio County during the 1920s. A lad caught a small green snake and kept it in his pocket until study time. He then kept looking up at a knothole in the ceiling. Other pupils whispered to ask what he was looking for and were told that he had seen a green snake look out from the knothole. Of course this intelligence spread over the room in a few minutes and pupils watched the ceiling anxiously. When all were gazing upward he released the snake, which started a stampede—boys squalled and ran, girls grabbed their skirts and jumped on desks while screaming at the top of their lungs. Finally the teacher restored some semblance of order. To settle the tale, the miscreant's seatmate told on him, which led to a good thrashing. The perpetrator (who wishes to remain anonymous) still derives much fun from the incident—even fifty years later.

The line between devilment and behavior that was recognized as meanness was also hard to determine. Pupils charged with the latter were considered to be "bad boys." Schools got reputations for the behavior of the pupils, sometimes good, sometimes bad. In both instances much of the behavior was neither good nor bad, just behavior of normal youngsters.

Probably only devilment was the behavior of the older boys in a certain Hart County school. There the big boys had learned to plague the young lady teacher by climbing up into the loft and refusing to come down for their classes. One day the county superintendent came unannounced while the boys were up in the loft. The alarmed teacher called up to warn them of the visitor's arrival, but in reply they only threatened her if she should tell on them. All through the superintendent's stay the teacher and the younger pupils were on edge, although they tried to carry on as best they could. Some of the bolder boys peered out from the loft above and behind the visitor with suppressed glee, especially when he inquired as to the whereabouts of any older boys of the school.

Accounts of devilment inevitably lead to others of punishment. Among the many accounts and stories of disciplinary problems and action by teachers, an occasional report stands out as distinctive. At the old Milledgeville common school in Lincoln County in the 1890s, discipline was no problem for the teacher until she had trouble with a trustee's son. The father then instructed the schoolmarm to send for him the next time the lad misbehaved. This she did. When the trustee arrived, he proceeded to give his son a very thorough whipping before the whole school. Either the thrashing, or the show of a solid front by teacher and trustee, or some other factor made a difference, because the young lad settled down as a model student. In his adult years he became a minister of the gospel and was often heard to say that the disciplinary action at the school that day marked the turning point of his life.

Perhaps the greatest number of human interest stories tends to cluster around the teachers and their relationships with pupils and others in the neighborhood. Teachers who were not interested in the pupils and their progress were quickly recognized by the children. One reminiscent remarked: "One of my teachers seemed to be teaching for what he got in the way of pay and that only. He would come late, leave early, would lay down on one of the long benches and take him a nap. We'd play sometimes an hour and a half out under the big beech tree in front—wouldn't wake him up for anything."

Other reports of teachers who did as little teaching as possible mentioned coming to school late, crocheting, embroidering, and doing other personal work during study time, and leaving the pupils unattended, but such references were relatively few.

Reports of teachers who were cross with pupils were somewhat more frequent. One of the reminiscents recalled a striking instance of such behavior after many years: "Although I was only seven, I could tell he didn't like children. He would call each child in the first and second grade to stand by him and read. Many of them didn't know a word. They repeated the words after him. Sometimes he would just say anything that came to mind and the child would repeat it. Then he would ridicule the child. How I did despise him for that. He didn't come back the next year. He left the profession, which was a blessing for the children." Other uncomplimentary tales told by pupils about teachers include rare references to schoolmasters who came to school drunk on homemade moonshine. A few reported teachers who tried to conceal "taking a chaw" during books time. Some recalled lazy mentors, and certain others remembered teachers who ridiculed pupils for doing poorly in their studies.

Teachers could be strict as long as they treated everyone the same under similar circumstances. But if they played favorites, there would be trouble. Many stories are told about ways devised to get even with teachers who were thought unfair and heartily disliked as a result. One bunch of fellows smeared the bell rope at just the right height with cow manure shortly before the dinner hour ended. The look of surprise on the teacher's face when he discovered his predicament was sufficient recompense for the thrashing given to all boys who could possibly have been in the plot, although it failed to disclose those who were responsible.

Stories that show why old-time scholars still fondly remember their good teachers also deserve mention, since there were many more good teachers than poor ones. Pupils liked teachers principally because of their general attitudes toward the children in their charge. They responded positively to those teachers who accepted them as persons and treated them fairly even if firmly.

Nevyle Shackelford remembered one of his teachers with great respect and affection. This lady was a very devout Christian and invariably opened school with a devotional period. One day she told the pupils about death—that angels came for people who died and took them to heaven. She made the prospect so realistic that young Nevyle was deeply concerned and could not keep back the tears. Seeing this the teacher came back, sat down by him, and asked what was the matter. Nevyle replied that he didn't want to go to heaven: "I just want to stay here with Mother and Dad."

Some of the best stories of old-time common school days may be found in the memoirs of one of the master spirits of the teaching profession, Ezra L. Gillis. After explaining that he originally started teaching in 1886 on a third-class certificate, intending to save money so that he could study law, he found during his first year that he enjoyed teaching. He began that first school with the resolution that he would do a good piece of work so that if he ever came back to that place he would not be ashamed to meet the people. The record showed that he put enough into it and received enough satisfaction to make a lifelong career as an educator.

The lives of innumerable teachers have been gladdened by the performance of bright pupils. One of Gillis's anecdotes tells of an astute observation by a pupil, William H. Townsend, who was destined to become an outstanding historian and lawyer. Gillis looked up from his desk one day and found young Townsend with his "Blue-Backed Speller," open to the alphabet, in one hand and a small dictionary in the other. He said, "Mr. Gillis, you know I have been working two weeks, all the time I could spare, and I haven't found a word in this dictionary that you cannot spell with that row of letters and I believe you can spell any word in that dictionary with those letters." Such research and reasoning on the part of a beginning pupil presaged his future success.[1]

The Friday afternoon exercises, so popular with pupils and patrons alike, were often the scene of funny happenings that were long remembered. One reminiscent recalled two such episodes:

Friday afternoons were set aside for spelling matches and recitations. It was compulsory for everyone to have a speech every Friday and some would recite the same one over and over. My favorite was, "Twinkle, Twinkle, Little Star." One day we all made it up among us to say this poem. After about five had said it, even the teacher had to laugh. Then she told us very emphatically that she wanted us to learn a new speech and let that one have rest.

I will never forget the speech of a little girl named Julia Bean. She walked up front and with all seriousness recited, "A black hen has red eyes," and sat down. You should have heard the laughing and clapping.

Normally the daily routine of the one-room school proceeded without unusual incident. But occasionally something happened that was highly dramatic. One such episode took place at the Sunnyside School in Marion County in the 1890s. An excellent and respected teacher, Miss Litsey, had the usual Friday afternoon spelling match well under way when the door flew open and a drunk burst in and started shooting. Children screamed and scrambled for safety. The man left hurriedly, but it took several minutes for the teacher to reassemble the children. The spelling match was never finished and for the first and only time, school was dismissed early. In view of the lack of injuries and the haste with which the intruder made his exit, people of the community believed him to have been less under the influence than he appeared and charged the deed to his general "low-down behavior and meanness."

Accounts of unusual incidents represent a wide variety of happenings. One elderly gentleman from Clay City, Kentucky, who attended a rural school in the 1890s, told of the pupils' interest in a hanging at the county seat some five miles away. Although the narrator was too young to join in the journey on that eventful day, most of the boys and some of the girls cut school and walked to town to witness the hanging.

Life in the old-time common school led to some rather embarrassing incidents. William H. Townsend related that during his common school days at Glensboro in Anderson County, the boys liked to climb up into the timbers of the bridge that spanned Salt River and carve their initials. All went well until a new boy enrolled in school. He made a good impression on the boys and, as a sign of his acceptance into the group, was invited to inscribe his initials. The lad hesitated; finally they discovered the reason for his reticence. They knew his first name started with A and his last name with S. They learned that his middle name also began with S. What was intended as a goodwill gesture turned into an embarrassing moment.

Accounts of teaching in Kentucky common schools seldom refer to anything that could be interpreted as sectarian instruction or efforts to indoctrinate pupils in matters of religion. On rare occasions, however, religious convictions led to controversy. In a central Kentucky school a teacher with strong Baptist beliefs expounded upon her doctrinal views at every opportunity, with special insistence upon immersion as the valid form of baptism. Noting this tendency, three children from the same family would raise questions calculated to use up time that would otherwise have been spent in recitation.

Real life stories of common school days and of the people who worked and played therein provide a rich resource for those who would study and appreciate the heritage of Kentucky today.

9

TO READ AND
REMEMBER

Few INSTITUTIONS have been remembered so fondly and described in such nostalgic terms as has the little one-room school. But the fond memories of the little white schoolhouse and its "dear old golden rule days" have a far more solid base than mere nostalgic recollections of former scholars. In its heyday in Kentucky, the common school was clearly recognized by many persons as an institution vital to the functioning and improvement of the society and the lives of the people. An editorial in the *Louisville Herald* (March 1, 1908) made this clear:

The rural school, next to the home, is the most vital force in the building up of the State. From these little centers of instruction, too often crude and comfortless, come the men and the women who will shape the future. It is to them we of a passing generation must commit the heritage that has come to us from other days. It is upon them that must devolve the burden of achieving for Kentucky that greatness among her sister Commonwealths of which we have dreamed as a goal but dimly seen.

There is inspiration in the little roughly constructed schoolhouse on whose hard benches sit the wide-eyed, mischief-loving children of today, conning the task, elementary from the standpoint of the college, but fraught with much of import in the

way of mental discipline and character development, fundamental to the larger life in older years. These places are not to
be despised, nor held in light esteem. They are sacred. Here
genius may be guided, here the flickering spark of some great
inspiration may be fanned into the flame of serious purpose;
while we still hold the tradition of that schoolhouse in which
Lincoln learned to spell, every nursery of knowledge must be
counted precious as a possible natal place of greatness. . . .

The rural school is the greatest asset that any state possesses.
It is possibly the asset which receives the least and the last con-
sideration.

Before the common school passed from the scene, there
were those who could see and deplore the evidences of
its demise. In 1906 one of the county seat newspapers
concluded an article titled "The Passing of the Country
School" with this eloquent statement:

But now the country school is going or has gone. Ghosts stand
here and there. Ancient landmarks dismantled, forlorn, mute
reminders of what has been. The life and associations that made
them what they were have flowed out into the highways of
traffic and business; but in all the noise and din there sometimes come memories of the school house on the hill. Ah,
thankful may you be if it was yours to go to the country school.
To those who have known it, it has incomparable values; it was
full of the initiative that makes life worth living.[1]

Although few people realized it at the time, the
agrarian society and the relatively self-sufficient life of
rural families were already in the grip of economic and
social forces that were to transform a way of life that had
prevailed through most of the state's history. One of the
visible phases of that transformation would be the decline and disappearance of the one-room neighborhood
schools.

Could the one-teacher schools have been saved? Any
effort to this end would have had to be made by the end of
World War I or the early 1920s, since the dynamic forces
that changed rural institutions were by then well under

way. A number of leaders and groups who appreciated the rural institutions and the agrarian economy of Kentucky had addressed themselves to the problem of revitalizing and improving the common schools in the first and second decades of the new century. Files of the state's metropolitan newspapers record significant and intelligent efforts to influence changes in the common schools with a view to strengthening the rural economy upon which the entire Commonwealth depended. Prominent in these efforts were the Kentucky Federation of Women's Clubs, the Kentucky Development Association, and the Committee on Education of the Louisville Commercial Club. Series of articles on the needs of the schools and of proposals for their improvement were published in the newspapers of the state. Model schools were constructed in both rural and urban settings, and there appeared to be effective liaison and cooperation among leaders interested in child labor problems, public health measures, and school improvement.

A number of public-spirited citizens visited other states and reported upon school programs and practices that seemed promising. Under this leadership School Improvement Leagues were formed in 103 of the 119 counties for the purpose of effecting improvements in the schools at the district and county levels. When Superintendent John Grant Crabbe organized and sent out speakers for the widely publicized Whirlwind Campaigns to arouse Kentuckians to the needs for improved schools in the fall of 1908 and summer of 1909, many of the 100 volunteers who took part were not from common schools. Agricultural leaders, judges and other public officials, members of women's clubs, journalists, clergymen, and higher education officials all gave unstinting support to the movement, which, by the way, was adapted and used in a dozen other states.[2] On Public School Sunday, June 27, 1909, nearly 5,000 ministers in the Commonwealth dealt with public education in their sermons to an estimated total of nearly half a million

Kentuckians. Crabbe reported that nearly 2,500 set speeches were delivered by the 100 speakers during the following week in over 100 counties. He was clearly scornful of the few county superintendents who were too busy to take part in the program, "planting sweet potatoes, fixing up their political fences, occasionally imbibing too much bad liquor, et cetera," but the great majority were praised for their efforts.[3]

Why did the one-teacher school decline and virtually disappear? The answer is multifaceted. At the close of World War I a popular song articulated the feelings of many persons, both within and without the armed services:

> How ya gonna' keep 'em
> Down on the farm,
> After they've seen Paree?

This same sentiment was repeated in myriad forms by thousands of Kentuckians in that same period, as the "Tin Lizzie," jobs in town, and numerous other new possibilities became available to those who had had enough of early rising, milking and feeding, and working all year to "sell your terbacker for whatever them buyers want to give you fer it."

The Whirlwind Campaigns and the concerted efforts of the Speakers' Bureau and local leaders in the counties made a spectacular impact upon the people of the Commonwealth, especially among the political leaders who were interested in education. But this was only the most visible and best publicized force at work for school improvement during the early decades of the century. Many people were concerned about the fate of the common schools.

Suggestions for the teaching of agriculture had been made at various times from the 1840s on by responsible spokesmen, among them the old *Louisville Journal* and other metropolitan newspapers, various farm journals, and the Grange in Kentucky. Proposals for the teaching of agriculture, domestic science, and manual arts in the common schools, as well as for the planting of school gardens, beautification of school grounds, and use of schoolhouses as community centers, were current during the decade before World War I, and all these suggestions were calculated to make the one-teacher schools functional in the improvement and strengthening of country life. The Kentucky Department of Education was recommending that agriculture, household arts, nature study, and the like be taught under the label of "General Exercises" several years before the General Assembly acted to add agriculture to the course of study.

Like many other movements, especially those that involve relatively complex concepts and relationships, this promising potential development got diluted and simplified. What was left was an emphasis upon consolidation of rural schools into multiroom centers and the resultant transportation of children. The interests of the school people and of farmers, who had long awaited mud-free roads to markets, met in an effort that was to change the appearance of the state's schools in the second quarter of the century. Unfortunately, pupils transported to early consolidated schools found little more than the program they had left in the rural common schools. The General Assembly soon added agriculture to the elementary school curriculum, but little attention was given to the new subject in the 1920s and the 1930s.

Was this then the end of the one-room school? An article that appeared in the December 24, 1974, issue of the *Christian Science Monitor* quoted the teacher of a one-room school in Vermont who believed that the little red schoolhouse was making a comeback: "Look at the trend to the open classroom. People think that's something new. It's not. It's just another name for the most obvious feature of the one-room school." The article further quoted David B. Tyack, a leading professor and author in the history of education in this country: " 'Once

93

we had it all: community control, non-graded primary instruction, cross-age tutoring, flexible scheduling, close parental involvement. Where? In the tens of thousands of one-room schools. . . . These days in mini-schools we try to recapture the humane scale of the country school, and with rediscovered techniques we try to loosen the rigidity of graded curricula and age-segregation. A once-discarded institution still can serve as a model for reform.' " School leaders, boards of education, and state officials still intent upon the effort to standardize all schools could profitably read some of the educational history of the Commonwealth as they ponder further the basic question posed by such statements as those quoted.

Aside from nostalgic remembrances and prophetic statements concerning the return of the one-room school, an essential question must be answered—"What heritage did the old Kentucky common school leave us?" Put differently, it might ask, "What useful lessons can we learn from the one-teacher school of our forefathers?"

Answers to these questions could take the form of a list of specific features and practices that could be viewed as strengths and weaknesses. Views and comments by old-timers who attended common schools emphasized the human features and individualized attention:

"We felt more like a family."

"We helped each other to learn."

"Pupils learned to work together."

"Older pupils helped the little ones."

"Strong on individual work."

"My teachers allowed pupils to proceed at their own rate."

"Pupils received much more attention from the teacher than is given today with all the modern methods and equipment."

"School was usually right pleasant. We worked and played and studied together in a right congenial way."

"Comradeship and fellowship have lasted through the years."

"Although the times were hard there was a closeness between teacher and pupils that we do not have today."

"It was the principal community activity and the poor and humble were as much a part as the learned and the property owners."

Another strong theme was the cooperation between parents and teachers, principally in the matter of support for discipline. Despite measures that today would be considered crude, even harsh, nearly all old-timers accepted correction and punishment as necessary for the establishment of good behavior. There can be little doubt that the strong rapport between most parents and teachers contributed significantly to this end:

"Our parents and teachers worked together, supported each other."

"We learned discipline at school and at home."

"We were taught manners and morals. Also, respect for the teacher."

"I liked the togetherness of the children and the respect for the teacher and other pupils. This is lacking in the schools of today."

Apparently the uncluttered environment and relaxed pace of the old-time rural school have come to be viewed as advantages when viewed in retrospect:

"Pupils enjoyed the simple way of life."

"Not so many outside activities that interfered with study and pupils could concentrate on scholastic work."

"Absence of severe social problems such as youth feel today in large schools meant pupils were freer of tensions and pressures and could study better."

Many of the former scholars had fond recollections of textbooks that played an important part in their education, particularly remembering the moral values that were stressed:

"I loved my old readers and have never forgotten many moral lessons they taught."

"When McGuffey's readers went out we lost something that was never replaced."

"I have never forgotten some of the pieces I memorized from my old readers."

And most people remembered the fun and pleasure they shared with schoolmates at playtime.

Disadvantages most frequently cited by old-timers included lack of time for covering so many subjects, the usual problems of too many pupils for the schoolroom and the need for individualized attention by the teacher, and the typical scarcity or absence of materials. None of these shortcomings will be considered peculiar to the one-room school by those who plan and practice education in our schools today.

Certain other problems that persisted throughout the history of rural common schools deserve to be placed in the record. Old-time common schools were plagued with poor attendance; they never appeared to have even one-half of the children of school age in attendance in a given year. A majority attended long enough to gain some simple skills, but left school early to go to work. Local school districts, for the most part, failed to assume their share of the support burden for their school. Trustees and taxpayers were willing to depend upon the meager funds available for distribution by the state from the School Fund rather than to levy taxes upon themselves. (This phenomenon is not unknown to educational and political leaders of recent times.) Rural common schools were handicapped for lack of better-educated teachers for much of their history. Whenever there was a shortage of teachers, it was always the rural common schools that had to make do with so-called emergency teachers.

One more persistent problem that affected the common schools must be mentioned, namely, plain old Kentucky-style politics and nepotism. The stories and allegations concerning these practices on the part of trustees, school board members, and superintendents would fill a large shelf of books. This problem has been reported in various areas and forms in the years since the one-room schools dominated the educational scene.

Perhaps the most significant weakness of the old-time common schools was the low ranking of Kentucky's educational system in certain studies and surveys around the close of the second decade of this century. One implication is clear: our old-time schools always had problems; our present schools face problems, some of which are rooted in our past history. The more we know about them, the better our chance of finding solutions.

A glowing tribute to the contribution of the old-time common school to the people of Kentucky would be an appropriate conclusion to this account of the one-room school in Kentucky. But whether this would do full justice to the subject is a question that gives pause to any conscientious writer. Perhaps two statements direct from the hearts of scholars who loved the old Kentucky common schools can say it best:

On the whole we were a fairly good group of children. I don't recall our teachers whipping or paddling many pupils. If we were punished at school we were punished at home. We were taught to respect our teachers and obey them. Children knew and loved each other. An air of sharing and fellowship was fostered.

The old schoolhouse has been torn down many years. It filled the need of that day. When we moved into the age of consolidation we gave up some things; however, we also gained much education-wise.

I am glad I had the privilege of attending a one-room school.

The old-time common school was truly a community institution, really treated people as individuals. I liked the old-time common school because we were like one big family. We loved each other and respected and loved our teacher. We had good times and learned much more than was in the books. We were taught "good manners," to be honest, kind to each other and pets, and high moral standards. These things were not forgotten.

For three centuries the one-room school served well the people of the United States. In our own Commonwealth its span of years has been approximately one-third of that time. Neither the people of the Republic nor the citizens of this Commonwealth can afford to skip the lessons that their educational history affords them. Eric Sloane reported the inscription of a colonial scholar on the flyleaf of a schoolbook in 1640 that deserves to be pondered and honored in our own time and place: "God give us grace to read and remember the truths herein."[4]

Notes

Chapter 1

1. William George Aaron, "History of Education in Adair County" (Master's thesis, University of Kentucky, 1933), p. 77.

2. Leonard C. Taylor, "History of Education in McLean County" (Master's thesis, University of Kentucky, 1940), p. 18.

3. Attella Ford Hartford, "School Days at Washington Station," *Ohio County News*, December 26, 1974. The account was originally written in 1956.

4. One provision of the 1830 Permissive School Act represents a first of its kind for the Commonwealth, possibly for a greater area: widows and *femmes soles* who owned property subject to taxation were permitted to vote in school district elections. The same provision was repeated in the Common School Act of 1838 and in subsequent school legislation. Later, in the 1890s, the General Assembly passed an act granting charters for the second-class cities (Covington, Lexington, and Newport) with the provision that women might vote in school elections. Little note was taken of this until politicians of Lexington induced the 1902 legislature to repeal the provision, arousing determined opposition by leaders of women's rights groups. These groups continued the fight for school suffrage until in 1912 the General Assembly enacted legislation that permitted women to vote in all school elections throughout the state.

5. Aaron, "History of Education in Adair County," p. 77.

Chapter 2

1. *Annual Report of Superintendent of Public Instruction, 1874* (Frankfort, 1874), p. 5.

2. Figures are from Superintendent's reports in *Kentucky Documents, 1882* (Frankfort, 1882), vol. 1, document 20, pp. 7–8; and *Kentucky Documents, 1901* (Louisville, 1901), vol. 3, document 5, p. 367, respectively.

3. *Public Education in Kentucky: A Report by the Kentucky Educational Commission* (New York, 1921); *The Educational System of Kentucky: A Report by the Efficiency Commission of Kentucky* (Frankfort, 1923).

4. *Public Education in Kentucky*, pp. 71–79.

5. Ibid., p. 83.

6. Ibid., p. 84.

7. *Educational Bulletin* of the Kentucky Department of Education, 1, no. 7 (September 1933): 25.

8. *Louisville Times*, February 2, 1911.

Chapter 4

1. *Kentucky Documents, 1851–52* (Frankfort, 1852), p. 201.

2. Gordon Wilson, *Fidelity Folks* (Cynthiana, Ky., 1946), pp. 193–240.

3. Ibid., p. 142.

4. Frances Rolston, "History of Education in Letcher County, Kentucky" (Master's thesis, University of Kentucky, 1939), pp. 16–17.

Chapter 5

1. William George Aaron, "History of Education in Adair County" (Master's thesis, University of Kentucky, 1933), p. 6.

Chapter 6

1. Several of the games and rhythmic activities that were widely used in the old-time common schools were included with instructions for players in the *Educational Bulletin: A Physical Training Manual for Kentucky Schools*, 5, no. 5 (July 1937).

2. This game first reported by old-time scholars from Anderson County and by a few others in the Bluegrass offers interesting speculation as to its currency over 3,000 miles and approximately 150 years from its obvious English origin before the Victorian era.

Chapter 7

1. Most references to this subject were made by former scholars in personal interviews, as only a few put comments on paper (which in itself provides a comment upon the period).

Chapter 8

1. Ezra L. Gillis papers, University of Kentucky Archives, Box 39, Folder 5, "Early Teaching Experiences," December 6–7, 1939.

Chapter 9

1. Quoted from the *Allen County Times*, in the *Louisville Times*, January 18, 1906.

2. *Report of the Superintendent of Public Instruction, 1907–09* (Frankfort, 1909), p. 82.

3. Ibid., p. 86.

4. Eric Sloane, *The Little Red Schoolhouse* (New York, 1972), p. 39.

A Note on Sources

SOURCES on the development of Kentucky's common schools range from general histories of the state to the files of county newspapers to the reminiscences of former pupils. Volume 2 of Richard H. Collins, *History of Kentucky* (Covington, Ky., 1874) contains a brief account of common schools to 1873. Various editions of William H. Perrin et al., *History of Kentucky* (Chicago, 1882), which features material about regional groups of counties, contain information about early schools and teachers of many localities. Perhaps the most readable account is in Thomas D. Clark's *History of Kentucky* (Lexington, Ky., 1950).

Several concise but general histories of public education in Kentucky are helpful sources. Despite the title, Alvin Fayette Lewis's *History of Higher Education in Kentucky* (Washington, D.C., 1899) treats the development of the common school system. Barksdale Hamlett, superintendent of public instruction from 1912 to 1916, published *History of Education in Kentucky* (Frankfort, Ky., 1914), based on reports of his predecessors in office. Two brief compilations from reports of the superintendents of public instruction since 1914 have brought Superintendent Hamlett's record forward through 1964. These are H. W. Peters, *History of Education in Kentucky, 1915–1940* (Frankfort, Ky., 1940), and Wendell P. Butler, *History of Education in Kentucky, 1939–1964* (Frankfort, Ky., 1964). Moses Edward Ligon's *History of Public Education in Kentucky* (Lexington, Ky., 1942) gives an account of the development and control of public education based upon constitutional and legal provisions for the schools from the beginnings to 1932. An excellent general work is Frank Lerond McVey's *The Gates Open Slowly* (Lexington, Ky., 1950). The most recent account is C. W. Hackensmith's *Out of Time and Tide* (Lexington, Ky., 1970), which briefly traces the evolution of education in Kentucky through the 1930s.

The most significant source of historical materials about the common schools may be found in the reports of the superintendent of public instruction. These have appeared annually, biennially, even quadrennially, sometimes incorporated in legislative documents and sometimes as separate publications. The whole series affords a comprehensive account of the establishment and operation of the common school system from 1838 to the present. In the early decades the superintendents used this medium to expound on ideas and measures calculated to improve the schools. Reports of the superintendents during the first two decades of this century provide significant evidence of constructive study and planning for schools to serve the agrarian society and people of the Commonwealth.

The Southern School Journal, published from the 1890s to the 1920s, is a veritable treasure trove of materials about Kentucky's schools. Its successor, *The Kentucky School Journal,* provided such a source until one-room schools went out of style.

Three major studies of Kentucky schools dealt with one-room schools at great length and influenced the making of educational policy in the period between the two world wars: General Education Board, *Public Education in Kentucky* (New York, 1922); Efficiency Commission of Kentucky, *The Educational System of Kentucky* (Frankfort, 1923); and the *Report of the Kentucky Educational Commission* (Frankfort, 1933). The latter report provided the basis for the new school code adopted by the General Assembly in 1934.

Candidates for master's degrees have written histories of education for nearly half of the counties in the Commonwealth. A good number of these provide relatively complete accounts of the operation of the common schools in their respective counties.

County seat newspapers provide one of the best sources of information about the common schools and teachers. Files of a given weekly often include stories on the annual Teachers' Institutes and notes about various schools sent in by teachers. Reports by the neighborhood correspondents often mention the local school or teacher. The history of education in the Commonwealth has been marked by a consistent degree of support for public schools on the part of the press, a fact that often goes unnoticed.

Relatively few books have dealt with the old-time common school in view of its character and the place it held in its rural neighborhood, but there are certain "classics" that depict early one-room schools and the life of pupils. Among these are Edward Eggleston's *The Hoosier School-Boy* (New York, 1891) and *The Hoosier Schoolmaster* (New York, 1871). A loving picture of a mountain blab school in the early years of the common school system may be found in chapters 3 and 4 of John Fox, Jr., *The Little Shepherd of Kingdom Come* (New York, 1911).

Books that deal with rural one-room schools and their role in the changing times of the past half-century are also relatively few. One of the best is Iman Elsie Schatzmann, *The Country School* (Chicago, 1942), which describes the rural schools of six nations. See part 2 for American rural schools. Another volume treating this period is the Committee on Rural Education's *Still Sits the Schoolhouse by the Road* (Chicago, 1943). A recent account by a great teacher who liked teaching in the one-room school suggests what should have happened in a large number of rural neighborhoods. See Julia Weber, *My Country School Diary* (New York, 1946). A fascinating recent book that reminds us of the heritage left by the one-room school is Eric Sloane's *The Little Red Schoolhouse*

(Garden City, N.Y., 1972). This volume deserves a place among books of the Bicentennial era.

But the single best-loved account of life in and around the one-room school is Jesse Stuart's *The Thread That Runs So True* (New York, 1949). This true story by one who attended the old one-room schools of Kentucky, and later taught in them, has received wide recognition, and its appeal has continued for more than a quarter-century.

Two former schoolhouses are open to the public as museums. These are the Cora Wilson Stewart Memorial, at Morehead State University, and the Granny Richardson Springs School, at Eastern Kentucky University.

Many of those who once attended Kentucky's one-room schools have contributed reminiscences of their school days. These are listed here chapter by chapter, in the order in which material they contributed appears.

Chapter 1: Leander Johnson, Cottle.

Chapter 2: Bert P. Easley, Lexington; W. R. Winfrey, Burkesville; Richard Shaw, Lebanon Junction; Mrs. Wade George, Versailles; Harrod Ward, Scott County.

Chapter 3: Mrs. Andrew Hatfield, Harlan County; Lee Dameron, Maysville; H. V. Noble, Sr., Covington; James E. Collins, Johnson County; Waller Williams, Lexington.

Chapter 4: Forrest Calico, Lancaster; Martha Riddell, Locust Grove.

Chapter 5: Alton Crisp, Allen; Virginia Shipp, Glendale; George W. Conway, Carroll County; Virginia Shipp, Glendale (again); Mrs. Billie Ray, Shelbyville; Sue D. Tabor, Mt. Washington; Hugh Lanham, Lebanon; Mr. and Mrs. Cecil Sammons, Meally; Joe T. Edwards, Danville; Christine Cruise, Shepherdsville; Tom Kurtz, Lancaster; William Browning, Viper; Tom Kurtz, Lancaster (again); Jesse Richardson, Hazard; Marjorie Drew, Lexington.

Chapter 6: Olive E. Barrett, formerly of Pike County; Mrs. Audrey H. Hubbs, Letcher County; William J. Jenkins, Letcher County; Kathryn Lytle, Bourbon County.

Chapter 7: Mr. and Mrs. Cecil Sammons, Meally; Nevyle Shackelford, Beattyville; Joe Mountz, Clay City; Mrs. Goldie Bell Young, Wayne County; Mrs. Billie Ray Pennington, Shepherdsville; Martha Graham, Franklin County; Mrs. Wade George, Versailles; Nancy Compton, Glendale.

Chapter 8: Martha Riddell, Locust Grove; Mrs. Jean Johnson, Glendale; Bertha Dishon Myers, Nicholasville; Alton Crisp, Allen; Virginia Shipp, Glendale; G. Dewey Newport, Covington; Nevyle Shackelford, Beattyville; Tom Parks, Jessamine County; Welby Rexroat, Lebanon Junction; Joe Mountz, Clay City; Mrs. Wade George, Versailles.

Chapter 9: Audrey B. Hubbs, Letcher County; Estelle Meyers, Shepherdsville.